D1187372

At Any Cost

At Any Cost

Anita Bryant
and Bob Green

Fleming H. Revell Company
Old Tappan, New Jersey

Unless otherwise identified, Scripture quotations are from the King James Version of the Bible.

Scripture quotations identified LB are from The Living Bible, Copyright © 1971 by Tyndale House Publishers, Wheaton, Illinois 60187. All rights reserved.

Scripture quotations identified NAS are from the New American Standard Bible, Copyright © THE LOCKMAN FOUNDATION, 1960, 1962, 1963, 1968, 1971, 1972, 1973, 1975 and are used by permission.

Scripture quotations identified PHILLIPS are from THE NEW TESTAMENT IN MODERN ENGLISH (Revised Edition), translated by J. B. Phillips. © J. B. Phillips, 1958, 1960, 1972. Used by permission of Macmillan Publishing Co., Inc.

Scripture quotations identified NEB are from The New English Bible. © The Delegates of the Oxford University Press and the Syndics of the Cambridge University Press, 1961 and 1970. Reprinted by permission.

Scripture quotations identified RSV are from the Revised Standard Version of the Bible, copyrighted 1946, 1952, © 1971 and 1973.

"National Security" by Dr. L. Nelson Bell reprinted from the *Presbyterian Journal,* Asheville, N.C.

Patrick Buchanan column reprinted by permission of the Chicago Tribune-New York News Syndicate.

Library of Congress Cataloging in Publication Data
Bryant, Anita.
   At any cost.

    1. Homosexuality—Moral and religious aspects—Christianity. I. Green, Bob, joint author. II. Title
HQ76.25.B79   261.8'34'157   79-9885
ISBN 0-8007-0940-3

TO our friends—
   who are not afraid to go to battle with us
   at any cost.

. . . When the enemy shall come in like a flood,
the Spirit of the Lord shall lift up a standard
against him.

Isaiah 59:19

Contents

At Any Cost

1
Standing for What Is Right

For the love of Christ constraineth us . . . .
2 Corinthians 5:14

Christians have values which are worth sharing. Those values embrace the plain statements of the Bible and dictate my responses to what happens to me and to those I love. The Bible is God's Word of guidance for the good of man. When situations which affect our lives run counter to what the Bible says, then we, as Christians, are obligated—if we are to remain true to God and what we believe—to stand for what is right.

The easy way out would be to retreat, to beat a hasty exit from that which smacks of controversy, and to withdraw from the ranks of the faithful. Such cowardice is not worthy to call itself Christian.

I would be a liar if I didn't tell you that the temptation exists. But I am not a quitter—never have been and, with God's help, never will be. By now the story of my life is familiar to most. It's been told in my previous books, and the media have picked up on it. The harsh realities of growing up in rural Oklahoma in a family separated by divorce, with all the trauma this brought, and early exposure to stage life contributed to my makeup and personality development. Classmates in high school considered me brassy and aggressive. I don't dodge such evaluations now, any more than I did then. I know where I've come from, why I am the way I am, and what my weaknesses are.

But I also know from where my strength comes. My favorite verse of Scripture explains it: "I can do all things through Christ which strengtheneth me" (Philippians 4:13).

More and more, however, I am beginning to realize that in and of myself I am no match for those who come at me from an entirely different stance—the secular world. In my efforts to try and cooperate with the media I have often come off looking the way they describe me to be—"a self-righteous, overzealous censor, using God as a cover, with a sneering air of superiority."

To avoid such criticism and casting a bad reflection on Christ and other Christians, I have attempted to give answers to reporters from different magazines and newspapers, but in so doing I have at times found myself walking in unfamiliar territory. I am much more at home performing a song or with my nose in my Bible or when I let the Word of God speak for me. I make no apologies for that. I would much rather be giving statements from the Bible which are part and parcel of my very existence. But I am criticized for this, the implication being that this is a cop-out.

Can you imagine what it's like to pick up a paper or magazine and read about yourself and see how stupid you are made to appear? Can you imagine the feelings that flood over me as I see an interview which I've granted in all good faith appearing in a magazine which we wouldn't bring into our home? How would you like to have everything you say subject to some reporter's pen and twisted and turned so that you come out looking like you are on a witch-hunt? Can you understand what it's like to see yourself on TV and wish you hadn't been put on the spot, having to answer a question the way you did? Many times I've experienced remorse because the message I tried to convey didn't come out the way I truly meant it. Sometimes I come away from such encounters feeling as though I've failed other Christians and the Lord.

I've certainly wanted to be a good spokeswoman for others who share our faith and our concern. I've prayed much. People wonder how I feel about all that's happened since January 1977 when we innocently stepped into the arena of world attention because of the stand we took on an issue that affected us as parents in Miami.

How do I feel? My feelings are a mixture of good and bad. Most of the time I'm really on top, and I could lick a tiger— happy, exuberant, grateful, excited about the future, in good spirits. At other times I'm more than merely "under the weather"—blue, depressed, worried, indulging in a "pity party," sad and down.

Now having said that, someone in the media will jump on it: "Christians aren't supposed to have such roller-coaster feelings." Fellow Christians have voiced their criticisms in the past also and will no doubt continue to do so. So be it. The Apostle Paul had his ups and downs. Even Jesus wanted to get away and be by Himself. We are not supersaints; we are fellow human beings. Paul explained it like this:

> We are pressed on every side by troubles, but not crushed and broken. We are perplexed because we don't know why things happen as they do, but we don't give up and quit. We are hunted down, but God never abandons us. We get knocked down, but we get up again and keep going. These bodies of ours are constantly facing death just as Jesus did; so it is clear to all that it is only the living Christ within [who keeps us safe] . . . .
>
> We boldly say what we believe [trusting God to care for us], just as the Psalm writer did when he said, "I believe and therefore I speak." . . .
>
> That is why we never give up . . . our inner strength in the Lord is growing every day . . . . So we do not look at what we can see right now, the troubles all around us, but we look forward to the joys in heaven which we have not yet seen. The troubles will soon be over, but the joys to come will last forever.
>
> 2 Corinthians 4:8–10, 13, 16, 18 LB

Bob and I have had our days of heaviness and heartache. But we've also experienced more strengthening of our faith, more assurance that we are in God's will, more answers to prayer, and more of the *true* joy of the Lord, than we've experienced before.

I've always been transparently open and honest in my books; I want this book to convey to you the full gamut of emotions I've experienced and what we've been through as a family. My feelings are not what counts; feelings fluctuate; they are unreliable barometers of what one thinks. But if because of our experience others can be helped and challenged to stand for what is right, then share we must. I keep coming back to words the Apostle Paul gave to young Timothy, his son in the faith.

Fight the good fight of faith, lay hold on eternal life, where-unto thou art also called, and hast professed a good profession before many witnesses.

1 Timothy 6:12

It is only as I've kept before myself these and other biblical injunctions that I've been able to keep on keeping on.

We've made mistakes; we've blundered at times. With these mistakes has also come personal repentance. Let me be quick to admit I've said things I shouldn't have said. Not deliberately, but more out of ignorance when being put on the spot and having to give a reply. But that's no excuse. We became involved, however, in an issue about which I personally knew very little—only that the Bible spoke against it just as it did other sins. There wasn't even time to try and inform myself at the outset. Since then I've read, studied, conferred with others, and have endeavored to become more knowledgeable.

The Bible says it so much better than I. All that we have read and heard has only served to confirm the fact that we were right in taking a stand. The Apostle Paul said:

We have been truthful, with God's power helping us in all we do . . . .

We stand true to the Lord whether others honor us or despise us, whether they criticize us or commend us. We are honest, but they call us liars.

The world ignores us, but we are known to God; we live close to death, but here we are, still very much alive. We have been injured but kept from death. Our hearts ache, but at the same time we have the joy of the Lord . . . .

2 Corinthians 6:7–10 LB

At the outset we were overly sensitive to criticism. At times we overreacted and let the media and our critics dictate to us to some degree. This was a cunning ploy on their part, and we fell for it. In so doing I came across as sounding like a militant fundamentalist waving a Bible in one hand and the flag in the other. I was unlearned in the ways of the media strategists. I was also gullible and naive, and to a great extent, I still am.

It is my nature to be full of fire. Most of my life I've been a go-getter, the original Unsinkable Molly Brown. I've been down, but never out. Even when I was very young, I was full of determination. I was a strong-minded, independent kid. Grandpa Berry used to call me "the brave one." But even with that kind of spunk, I've not been fully prepared to stand up to all that's come at me since the Miami referendum vote.

Through all that's happened, I've sought to bring my nature under the control of the Holy Spirit. I want that fire in my temperament to come through in loving ways. I want to motivate people in love. The hardest thing I've had upon me has been the constraint of Christ.

That needs explaining. My basic nature is to fight back. There are times when I would like to belt people. That doesn't sound very ladylike, I know. My dad was a real roustabout—working in the Oklahoma oil fields—and I must have inherited some of his tenacity and stubbornness. Every so often, it comes to the fore. Then I have to submit to the inner working of God through His Holy Spirit who checks my natural impulses. I sense Christ's love, and I know that the only way He will be honored is if I hold myself in restraint. It is as if He is telling me to stand firm, to be strong, but to respond in love. The media misinterpret it as weakness and make fun of it. The Bible explains it like this:

For the love of Christ constraineth us . . . .

2 Corinthians 5:14

The Living Bible says:

Whatever we do, it is certainly not for our own profit, but because Christ's love controls us . . . .

The word that has lodged in my thinking and has dictated my responses has been the word *constraint*. While the world hammers at me and some Christians misunderstand and misinterpret what I say or I am quoted out of context, I have had to submit to that inner constraint.

I must confess that at times I bury my face in my hands and weep. It has been a lonely time in my life. And it is not over. Yet, I would not change places with anyone else. I know I'm where God wants me, doing what He expects of me.

The Bible offers reassurance. Jesus was misunderstood. Jesus knew what it meant to be lonely in a crowd. He also knew the feeling of being alone. I am sure that Jesus was totally misunderstood when He showed strength and exerted power and authority in purging the Temple. We have the account in John's Gospel, chapter two.

Jesus was angry. To many this is the most astonishing event in Jesus' life. Weren't His emotions always under control? Were they out of control when He strode boldly through the Temple with a whip in His hands, chasing out the money changers? Jesus knew exactly what He was doing. He knew His actions would result unquestionably in definite hostility toward Himself. Here we see Jesus as He embodies the very fury of God—righteous indignation; yet, this is also love in action.

Jesus upon earth was God in the flesh. As our heavenly Father, He responded to His enemies and critics when He saw things happening that adversely affected His earthly children. I have thought of that many times especially when people have said or implied that I have come on too strong. Yet if my motivation had not been of love, I could not have stood as I did. It has only been the grace of God that has pulled me through.

And so the pressure from both the church and those outside the church has been felt. It is something that I must live with. While I have endeavored at all times to show compassion and understanding to the homosexual, the necessity still exists to hold to the highest possible standards of the Christian life. It is like walking a tightwire. The need for balance is all-important.

I have found so much in Paul's writings that say exactly what's on my heart. After studying and coming to recognize the kind of culture into which he came with the message of Christ, I better understand why he said what he did. Paul's stance has become our stance:

So everywhere we go we talk about Christ to all who will listen, warning them and teaching them as well as we know how . . . .

Colossians 1:28 LB

There are books out now, and there are those making speeches who accuse me of putting down homosexuals and making them out to be second-class citizens. They say I have shown no compassion to homosexuals. We are said to be giving out hysterical misinformation and making judgments and pronouncements without knowing or understanding what we are talking about. They say we are lacking in understanding. We are labeled as generating hatred and using Christianity as a way of discrimination. We are said to have tremendous hostility and hatred for the homosexual.

I cannot tell you how this saddens me. I truly do love the

homosexual, and all sinners for that matter. It has been said that I am a one-issue person, which is not true. I hate "sins" in the plural just as Billy Graham, Oral Roberts, and other public religious figures have expressed. I have spoken out on the issue of homosexuality because it is the one we were confronted with. I have said it hundreds of times, and I'll go on saying it. I love the homosexual too much not to tell him the truth. I love these people enough to care about where they're going to spend eternity. And I love them enough to want to do something to help them.

I have often emphasized that when we come to Christ for forgiveness and salvation, we come away as "former somethings." There are some who come away as former alcoholics, adulterers, thieves—sinners, each of us, regardless of what we once were. That includes me.

Christ's purpose in coming into this world was to offer salvation to the *admitted* sinner. So none of us who claim to be Christians can boast of any righteousness by our own merit. We are *all* just sinners saved by God's grace. But the important thing to make sure of is that we have seen and acknowledged our sin, that we have turned from it and are no longer practicing it. When I repeat what the Bible says about sin—including homosexual acts—and emphasize that God calls for repentance (which means a feeling of sorrow and changing one's ways), I do so with compassion. Deliberate and unrepented sin of *any* kind is contrary to the will of God, and until we admit *and forsake* our sin we cannot experience the forgiveness of God in Christ.

Such statements on my part do not reveal a poverty of compassion. What my critics' statements reveal is the depths of depravity to which the human mind will go to justify and hang onto one's self-centered sexuality. The biblical truths of which I speak do not originate with me. This call for repentance is not my idea. My source book of truth is the Word of God.

The Old Testament prophet Isaiah, with the promises of God as yet unfulfilled, called his hearers to faith, and to repentance. It was a stirring plea then; it still is:

Seek ye the Lord while he may be found, call ye upon him while he is near: Let the wicked forsake his way, and the unrighteous man his thoughts: and let him return unto the Lord, and he will have mercy upon him; and to our God, for he will abundantly pardon.

Isaiah 55:6, 7

The simplicity of that really does not require an explanation. Yet there are those who would alter such teachings to fit their sin bent. Such deceptive rationalization is nothing short of religious blasphemy. I can continue to do nothing less than what the Apostle Paul did, even though his life was in great danger. Paul confidently declared that he never shrank from telling the truth. Paul told it like it was. Let it never be said that Anita Bryant wasn't willing to tell it like it is.

I have had one message for Jews and Gentiles alike—the necessity of turning from sin to God through faith in our Lord Jesus Christ.

Acts 20:21 LB

Sinners still need a Saviour. God's Word hasn't changed.

2
No Turning Back

A journey of a thousand miles begins with a single step.

LAO-TSZE

At the conclusion of the Dade County campaign to repeal the so-called "gay rights" ordinance in Miami, I hoped we'd be able to settle back into a more normal routine and the way of life to which we were accustomed. We recognized the necessity of some kind of ongoing work to protect America's children, and we were already somewhat organized and prepared to share the benefit of our experience, but I was inwardly hoping that Anita's involvement in particular could be less.

While the media were saying, "The Florida Sunshine Girl is going national with her attack on homosexuals," I was counting on time to come to our rescue and make it possible for my wife to gracefully bow out of the scene, if not completely, at least becoming much less visible and vocal. But such was not to be the case. As I've looked back over what's happened and have tried to analyze the scene, I have come to the conclusion that the reason we are still in the forefront of the continuing homosexual saga is because God intends for it to be that way.

There will be those who take exception to this, including the reviewer of *The Anita Bryant Story* who ridiculed the idea that we (or anyone else for that matter) could have the ear of God. This reviewer complained that she and others "are still spending our years struggling with what is right and wrong and various nuances

21

of same." I'd have to say her assessment of her own plight is accurate. The reason Anita can speak with such boldness and talk about her relationship with God is because she's not struggling like that. Anita and I have accepted the Bible's teachings on what is right and what is wrong, and we are not ashamed to stand up for what is right at any cost.

As the letters, telegrams, phone calls, and messages continued to pour in assuring us of the prayerful and loving concern of the citizens of this country, I began to realize that God was showing us through these people that there was to be no turning back.

Anita reminded me of the teaching in the Gospel of Luke. As Jesus was calling forth His first disciples, the story is told of two men who wanted to continue with their own plans before abandoning all to follow Jesus. Jesus' reply demonstrated the need for total abandonment to do His bidding. On that day so long ago, it is recorded for *our* learning that Jesus said, "Anyone who lets himself be distracted from the work I plan for him is not fit for the Kingdom of God" (Luke 9:62 LB). Anita said, "Bob, we've put our hand to the plow."

We sure had! Many times my thoughts have shot back to that day in the courthouse when Bob Brake, a local attorney and a former Dade County commissioner, stepped up to Anita after the vote and said, "Would you head up an organization to defeat this ordinance, Anita?" Anita turned to me, and we conferred briefly. We decided she should accept the challenge.

A letter that is representative of the many that come to our attention roused us to gear up for what lay ahead. It came from a woman in Cleveland who wrote after Anita had performed at a concert there.

I pray to God that the Christian community can match your courage and rally to the common cause that binds us all. Together, with God's help, we *can* change the present sad shape of our country for the better.

We have gone so far astray from the religious principles

and ideals on which our country was founded. It will be a
long, difficult, painful journey back, but as the Chinese prov-
erb says, "A journey of a thousand miles begins with a single
step." Anita, you have taken that initial step for all like-
minded Christians around the world. Now, it is up to us to
join you in one long parade of Christian soldiers who believe
that God, not man, is the molder of the future. Knowing how
much you and your family have already been through, and
how much you will have to face in the future for your beliefs,
I want in some small way to comfort and reassure you that
you do not stand alone. Do not be afraid to stand on the firing
line for God's cause. With your great faith, Anita and Bob,
you have set an example for the rest of us to follow.

Letters like that, coupled with our own deep feelings and concern, helped us to see that we could not get away from the need
for continued involvement in matters that affect the present and
future well-being of ourselves, our children, and others.

One day Anita said to me, "Bob, we can't go back anymore
than an infant can go back into the womb." I knew she was right.
Together we turned our attention to the organization which had
formed as a result of the Miami issue. Save Our Children was the
name originally chosen to serve as the umbrella for our efforts. It
was a local organization which existed to meet those immediate
needs in Dade County. However, as a result of a suit by the
Connecticut-based Save the Children child-assistance agency, we
were enjoined by law from using that name in a national venture.
Rather than become involved in a lengthy, time-consuming, and
costly legal battle, we decided to abandon that name and instead
chose the name Protect America's Children, Inc.

On the Los Angeles radio station KABC talk show with host
Michael Jackson, Anita explained very well what our intentions
were with Protect America's Children. She said that because of
our concern for communities which have turned to us for help and
information, we would provide seed money and the expertise

others need as they confront similar ordinances.

As the work has developed, we have envisioned seven categories of action: informational, educational, legal, moral, organizational, political, and legislative.

It has been a great encouragement to discover that the so-called "straight" silent majority is no longer willing to remain silent. There are others who are rising to protect their children, too, just as we did in Dade County. There are many things that pose threats to our children and to family life. There's child pornography, child abuse, drugs, alcohol, abortion, and of course, those who would try to foist upon an unsuspecting community what the homosexuals did in Miami. We need to be awakened to these things. Protect America's Children exists to help put a stop to evils in our society that are threatening our children today.

We realize that a secular religion called *humanism*—the view that man, rather than God, is the center of the universe—has taken over public education from coast to coast and is using school textbooks and sex-education classes to push homosexuality as being perfectly normal and proper. In view of this, we are working for a return to the "old-fashioned" idea of recognition of God in our schools. We are also deeply concerned about the evils of the so-called Equal Rights Amendment (ERA) and all the unrestrained sex and violence on television.

Wherever we go we find that people are asking: "Has America lost its sense of morality?" There is certainly much evidence that the principles upon which our forefathers founded this nation are no longer being followed. It is a sad and tragic commentary that we can no longer ignore. To do so is to invite our own national demise.

I've noted that some of the more toughened columnists are joining the ranks of those who wish to be counted as standing in opposition to the moral landslide taking place in America. One such reporter even questioned whether this moral erosion could be traced to a sort of cop-outism on the part of church leaders unwilling to face up to the issues. He asked, "Have we been too easy on drunkards, gamblers, homosexuals, and Lesbians?'' He decried the silence on the part of leaders who have failed to speak out against rampant dishonesty, promiscuity, and perversion. This from a columnist *not* noted for any religious fervor! I had to applaud when I read his comment that simply reaffirming opposition to sin doesn't quite hack it. Protect America's Children will do more than call attention to such sin.

When Brother Bill, Reverend William Chapman, our pastor at the Miami church we attend, announced his decision to go into full-time evangelistic work, we, as well as other members in our church, were pretty shook up. We had come to depend upon his counsel, and his leaving would create a gap in our lives. At first Anita rebelled. She was shocked, and then she was remorseful. I marvel at my wife's inner stability and her wisdom at such moments. ''Well, Bob,'' she said, ''I guess God is trying to tell us that we must not expect from others what only He is capable of giving, and that we must not make excessive demands of others. We need the counsel of Brother Bill and others like him, but in the final analysis each of us personally must be led by the Spirit of God.''

But Brother Bill's help was immediately needed. Someone had to respond to the cries for help from cities faced with the same kinds of problems we confronted in Miami. Would he go on fact-finding missions for us? Yes, he would.

We were all in agreement. This is what Protect America's Children was all about—being able to work through God's people to bring our nation back to its moral standards and Bible-based laws. Brother Bill would go and help set up local task forces which could provide the kind of help needed to fight immoral laws.

Wichita, Saint Paul, Seattle, New York, and others—the calls for help came in faster than we had anticipated. America's cities are facing the question: Should homosexuality be approved as a respectable and acceptable life-style? Citizens are being called upon to make a decision: accept the homosexual life-style as an operational part of their schools, churches, businesses, and government, or reject it as immoral behavior.

Protect America's Children was contacted in early February 1978 by Reverend Richard Angwin, a pastor at Saint Paul's Temple Baptist Church. He explained how he led a small group of citizens to get more than seven thousand names on a petition to repeal the "special privileges" ordinance for homosexuals.

He told how his home had been entered, a bloody ax left on his daughter's bed, human waste dumped on the floors, their pet poodle blown to bits, and his Bibles torn up and stomped on so hard you could see the footprints.

Anita and I were horrified! Reverend Angwin related how citizens, politicians, and ministers had come to him secretly and asked him to provide leadership to begin a petition drive to repeal the "gay rights" laws in Saint Paul. "This was indecency telling decency to stay in the closet," Reverend Angwin stated.

We sent Brother Bill to Saint Paul where he was met by Reverend Angwin and Senator Mike Menning, a Minnesota state senator. Brother Bill preached, and NBC- and CBS-TV affiliates filmed the service. The city of Saint Paul provided police protection—plainclothesmen as well as uniformed. Conferences with local pastors and civic leaders were held, and there were newspaper and television interviews. Time was spent in educating the concerned citizens of Saint Paul who would be involved as to what they could expect. Literature and materials were shared with them, and Brother Bill helped lay the groundwork for the overall campaign strategy which they would need to follow. Seed money was desperately needed, and Protect America's Children supplied initial funds.

The rest is now history. Saint Paul became the second city to rescind a "gay rights" provision by an overwhelming vote. Columnist Patrick Buchanan reported, "Like the Union Army at the second Manassas, the gay-rights movement has been routed anew in its second collision with Christian fundamentalists." He accurately reported the outrage of the National Gay Task Force and its co-directors, Jean O'Leary and Bruce Voeller, who stated: "We

are outraged that a majority of misinformed voters have once
again denied civil rights to a group of American citizens . . . ."
Buchanan, with incisive reporting, made this analysis of the
Saint Paul scene:

> Meaning no disrespect to Bruce and Jean, the voters of St.
> Paul are not misinformed. Nor was their decision a denial of
> any legitimate civil right.
>
> The voters considered the claims of the militant homosex-
> uals and decided that: (A) Parents and public school officials
> should retain the right to set standards of personal conduct
> for teachers. (B) Landlords may take into consideration the
> life style of prospective tenants. (C) Lawyers, accountants
> and businessmen may decline to hire employees whom they
> feel will leave a negative impression upon prospective
> clients.
>
> Hardly a reactionary lot, considering the liberals Min-
> nesota sends to Congress, the people of St. Paul simply de-
> termined that the traditional prerogative of school officials,
> landlords and employers should be maintained.
>
> As citizens, homosexuals, militant or not, are certainly
> entitled to the same constitutional rights and protections as
> every American. If those rights were at issue, St. Paul's vote
> would have gone the other way.
>
> But constitutional rights are not what the homosexuals are
> demanding. Nor are they asking a measure of compassion
> and understanding. What the National Gay Task Force seeks
> is to unfurl and elevate a banner of homosexuality—and
> force the rest of us to fire a 21-gun salute. They ask not
> acceptance or tolerance, but approbation and celebration of
> gay pride.
>
> They wish to flaunt what their fellow citizens consider to
> be depraved or sick or sinful behavior—and then be exempt,
> by law, from any social or economic sanction. They want to
> flout the customs, mores and standards of society—and re-
> main immune from social reprisal.

St. Paul said no.

What is ludicrous about this human rights campaign is the comparison the militant gays constantly draw with the black struggle for civil rights.

Black Americans had no choice in the color of their skin. Homosexuals, no matter their sexual orientation, do have a choice in their public behavior. For a century, blacks who worked hard, obeyed the law, paid their dues to society, were still barred by color from jobs, schools, restaurants, neighborhoods.

For two centuries, however, homosexuals, who did not openly defy the standards of this once-Christian country, have risen to the apex of their professions in business, journalism, politics and law.

To equate the black struggle with the gay struggle is thus to equate history with farce.

As for Bruce and Jean, they should count themselves fortunate it was the city of St. Paul—not the apostle—who was passing judgment last week.

Earlier in 1978 we appeared with evangelist Cecil Todd of Revival Fires, Joplin, Missouri, in a "Revive America Rally" in Wichita, Kansas. We had a press conference and met with some of the local concerned citizenry and the executive-board members of a group called Concerned Citizens for Community Standards. Brother Bill met later with several church groups who joined together—Protestants, Catholics, Jews, and Mormons—all united to uphold the biblical standards of morality in compassionate and caring ways. The same efforts were put forth in Wichita as in Saint Paul, with Protect America's Children providing ten thousand dollars in seed money.

We were much impressed with Reverend Ron Adrian, pastor of Glenville Baptist Church in Wichita, and president of Concerned Citizens for Community Standards. With leadership such as this waging battle against militant homosexuals in cities in similar plights across the country, we dare to believe that America can be spared the fate that befell ancient Rome.

Wichita voters overturned the "gay rights" ordinance by a resounding five-to-one margin. We issued a statement to the press wherein Anita congratulated the citizens of Wichita for this moral victory. "It is now obvious that the will of the American people is to return this country to pro-family Bible morality.

"Hopefully, the White House will be challenged by this and similar victories in Miami and Saint Paul to take a more consistent stand for those values that made America a great nation."

A two-to-one winning edge was scored in the Eugene, Oregon, vote in late May 1978. Another congratulatory telegram was sent: "Let us continue to reach out in godly love to all homosexuals who want deliverance, while opposing at the threshold every attempt of the militant homosexuals to represent their life-style as 'normal' and to impose it on us and our children."

At least thirty-seven municipalities in the United States have homosexual-rights ordinances. Protect America's Children stands ready to help other cities which sense the need to repeal such ordinances. Richard Whitcomb, in a Miami-TV News Commentary, stated that to determine one's *own* life-style is a "right." But to demand that others legally condone it is a "wrong."

More and more serious-thinking journalists and commentators are making statements like this. Charles Reese, writing in the Orlando, Florida, *Sentinel Star,* states, "Homosexual rights is one of the phoniest issues around and the people see through it, if most of the national pundits do not." He emphasized that as minorities go, homosexuals are among the most affluent and least discriminated against. "After all, who's been blacklisted? Not the homosexuals. Anita Bryant."

Reese points out something that is often overlooked.

Anita Bryant has been treated unfairly by most of the media. She has been accused of attacking homosexuals when in fact it was the homosexuals who initiated the contest. She merely responded. Secondly, she has been pictured as some wild, intolerant person when, in fact, she is not.

Much was made of a recent statement in which she said she believed those who were not "saved" would go to hell. The implication was that this position was unique to Anita Bryant.

That is not true. That is the basic doctrine of a number of Christian denominations and it used to be the basic doctrine of practically all of them . . . . It is a position that has nothing to do with Anita Bryant . . . .

The public, always more sensible than the media, is siding with Anita Bryant against license and for those ideals which promote family and lasting relationships.

The queer thing is how few public allies she has. Which proves, I suppose, that while homosexuality is a form of deviant behavior, it is at least more readily found than courage.

Someone wrote a letter to the editor of the Phoenix, Arizona, *Gazette* in which he called attention to Ezekiel 33:7–9. The writer stated: "Not only does Anita have a right to speak out on things that are wrong, it is her responsibility. And that goes for all of us."

I looked up those verses and they really pack a wallop. If we really believe the Bible, and we want to stand on the side of doing what is right and required of us as Christians, then the implications of these verses puts a tremendous responsibility upon all of us.

"Now as for you, son of man, I have appointed you a watchman for the house of Israel; so you will hear a message from My mouth, and give them warning from Me.

"When I say to the wicked, 'O wicked man, you shall surely die,' and you do not speak to warn the wicked from his way, that wicked man shall die in his iniquity, but his blood I will require from your hand.

"But if you on your part warn a wicked man to turn from his way, and he does not turn from his way, he will die in his iniquity; but you have delivered your life."

NAS

3

The Day of the Comfortable Christian Is Over

Now what use is it . . . for a man to say he "has faith"
if his actions do not correspond with it? . . .
James 2:14 PHILLIPS

When we started in January 1977, I didn't realize the Dade County situation would lead to a national organization to help other cities. The response has been staggering.

I pray that when you, the reader, read news articles or hear news about my public and private life, you will not let the liberal press slant your view. At a press conference during the time of writing of this book, an editor of a religious magazine, in posing a question to me, stated that he didn't necessarily agree with my "theological position." I wanted to say, "And how do you and I differ?" I wanted also to ask him if he had read *The Anita Bryant Story* which tells our side of the homosexual story. I could understand why he felt we differed if all he based his knowledge on was what he'd read in the newspapers and magazines. Reporting has been erroneous, and things I've said, quoted out of context.

The exciting and positive thing about all that has happened is that grass-roots people, the clergy, civic leaders, and legislators are looking at the homosexual issue now. They are discussing it and other moral issues confronting this country. There has been an awakening. Whereas before it was underground, now it is out in the open. For me, if I did nothing else but help *one* individual, it would be worth it all. In the final analysis, we are accountable to God.

I may not have the media or the entertainment industry backing me, but I know I do have the backing of the majority of the American people. It is not anything I sought or asked for; but what the militant homosexual community has meant for evil, God has meant and has used for good. And that is biblical.

The story is told in Genesis. Joseph's brothers were jealous of him. With hatred burning in their hearts, they stripped him of his coat, cast him into a pit, then sold Joseph to their enemies. The Bible says that "the Lord was with Joseph." In process of time he rose to a position of prominence in the house of a ruler in Egypt. In God's providence, many years later a famine in Canaan sent Joseph's brothers to Egypt in search of corn, and they ended up in the presence of Joseph. Joseph treated them well and later revealed his identity to them. In a moment of emotional confrontation, "Joseph told them, 'Don't be afraid of me. Am I God, to judge and punish you? As far as I am concerned, God turned into good what you meant for evil, for he brought me to this high position I have today so that I could save the lives of many people. No, don't be afraid . . .' " (Genesis 50:19–21 LB). And we are told that Joseph spoke very kindly to them, reassuring them.

There will be those who will jump on that and say, "Anita Bryant claims she is some kind of saviour." But no, that is not what I am saying. Let there be no mistake; I recognize that God has been in control from the outset and what was intended for evil by men with wrong intent, God has turned and used for great good. Now it is our God-given responsibility as Christians to resist deliberate attempts by militant homosexuals and Lesbians and their sympathizers to legalize that which is blatantly sinful. In particular, we must guard against the church's sanctioning, in the name of compassion, that which the Bible declares to be sinful. Such movements are afoot. There are well-known church leaders who are saying the church must counter my statements. One such woman leader stated, "Society doesn't have enough knowledge about homosexuality to consider it without being judgmental. This is one of those areas that we don't know enough about now. I don't know why, but God makes people this way, and I know He loves them, and I don't feel like being judgmental about it . . . . This is a misuse of religion that we have had through all of the centuries about anything we don't like. In terms of loving people, I think it's a terribly unloving way to behave."

God makes people this way . . . . What could be more erroneous than to blame God for the sin of homosexuality? No one can lay that charge to the Almighty. Research data consistently show that homosexuals must make a choice whether to act out their sexual preference or to keep it under control. Jerry Kirk in his book *The Homosexual Crisis in the Mainline Church* states that righteousness, not research, will decide where the church must stand. As of now the claims of scientists and researchers are contradictory. Either the church stands on the claims of the Word of God and faces up to the fact that God calls for moral responsibility, or it will be held accountable for failure to hold up the standards of righteousness.

It is hoped that more churches will adopt resolutions like the one passed by commissioners to the 190th General Assembly of the United Presbyterian Church meeting in San Diego in May 1978. Their resolution stressed that "the New Testament declares that all homosexual practice is contradictory to Christian faith and life," and that "our present understanding of God's will precludes the ordination of persons who do not repent of homosexual practice." It said that ministers are not free to adopt a "lifestyle of conscious, continuing and unresisted sin." It called on the church to combat "homophobia," the fear and hatred of homosexuals, and urged congregations to accept as members homosexuals who are committed to Christ and are willing to examine their condition in the light of Christian teaching.

The world's standards are not the Christian's standards. They never have been nor will they ever be acceptable to those of us who are practicing Romans 12:2: "And be not conformed to this world: but be ye transformed by the renewing of your mind, that ye may prove what is that good, and acceptable, and perfect, will of God."

I am accountable to my Maker to live responsibly. The fact that my views on responsible living have thrust me into the limelight means that I have as much right—no, I have a moral obligation if I am to remain true to myself and to the Lord—as the homosexual or homosexual supporter to state my views. That these views conflict with the secular world's views should come as no surprise to either the church or those who claim no religious ties. I want to be totally in God's will and obedient to Him. God's timing is never wrong. In His providence, He has brought the issue of homosexuality to the attention of the world through all that has happened. So long as the homosexual is pampered by fence-straddling Christians, the homosexual is without hope. We do the homosexual no favors when we tolerate this sin on the basis of "Christian love."

At a Word of Life conference at Schroon Lake, New York, where I performed in concert, I heard these words: *"What God's holiness condemns, His love can never embrace."* Let me tell you, those words have lingered in my thinking and reinforced my conviction that if you really love someone, you will speak the truth to him in love particularly when his very soul is in danger of eternal separation from a holy God.

John Hansen, a former homosexual now being used wonderfully by the Lord, was in our home for a two-day brainstorming session. For twenty years he was a practicing homosexual. At the very brink of suicide, in total despair, he had a life-changing encounter with God. Today he stands tall and true to the Bible. "Stand next to the Truth, and you will stand too," he asserts.

John's views on *love* are worth examining. John says the "gay" people define love in deceptive terms with semantics that are the devil's tool. "Love is a verb," he declares, "an action word. Love is always treating someone else so that his ultimate best interest is your first concern, and then your interests are automatically taken care of."

The illustration may seem too simple to some, but it is an apt illustration. If I saw a man drowning, and I had it within my power to rescue that man, but I turned my back and walked away, what kind of a person would I be? That's love in action? Just so, I see the homosexual as a victim who needs help. I have it within my power to hold out to the homosexual, in Christlike compassion, that which will rescue him from his condition now, and will save him from eternal punishment. My way of showing love may not necessarily be the same as someone else's, but who is being judgmental when they accuse me of unloving behavior?

I read the anguished letter which a mother wrote to a well-known columnist. She told of her discovery of a letter written by her son to the columnist. In the letter he confesses he is a homosexual and wants to come out of the closet. The mother wrote: "I felt as if my insides had dropped out." The plea is made for the columnist *not* to print the boy's letter, and she then signs her letter, "Reeling and trying to hang on."

My heart ached for days for that mother, and I still find myself anguishing with her. I owe it to that mother, and others like her, to continue, so long as God gives me strength, to speak the truth in love. I know there is help and hope for the homosexual sons and Lesbian daughters of mothers such as this. The homosexual is a captive of his fleshly desires which the Bible clearly labels immoral and therefore sinful. With other caring Christians I stand ready to love the homosexual who admits that he too is a sinner in need of God's forgiveness and saving grace.

Evangelist Cecil Todd says he learned a long time ago not to let the dissenters be deciders. That phrase sticks with me. Jerry Kirk says instead of our witnessing to the culture, we have let the culture witness to us. These two are saying the same sort of things. I cannot get away from the implications of these and similar observations on the part of others. I have been greatly helped by the counsel of men of this stature.

I have observed that many people tend to let fear rule their lives rather than to ask God to give them the courage to match their inner convictions. They capitulate to the vocal unafraid minority—the dissenters—and allow them to ramrod decisions through local legal channels that can have only far-reaching adverse effects. They are afraid to get involved, to give up some of their leisure time, to subject themselves to possible criticism—and so they allow the world to squeeze them into this mold.

Ed Rowe, executive director of Protect America's Children and Anita Bryant Ministries, in his book *Save America* explains that belief in the Bible does not necessarily result in effective action. The great majority of Christians are interested only in the personal dimensions of Christianity. Theirs is an egocentric faith; the big *me* is prominent. Their faith begins with Christ and ends with self. The tragedy of our time is the failure of so many sincere Christians to apply the truths and principles of the Bible faithfully and consistently throughout the whole spectrum of sociopolitical reality.

As this relates to the homosexual and his problem, I would urge that we Christians stand together united against this evil tide which is a threat to the sanctity of the church and our homes and communities. We need to remind ourselves of Ephesians 2:3–5:

> All of us used to be just as they are, our lives expressing the evil within us, doing every wicked thing that our passions or our evil thoughts might lead us into. We started out bad, being born with evil natures, and were under God's anger just like everyone else.
>
> But God is so rich in mercy; he loved us so much that even though we were spiritually dead and doomed by our sins, he gave us back our lives again when he raised Christ from the

dead—only by his undeserved favor have we ever been saved—

LB

The problem is that we are intimidated. We are allowing the dissenters to control the media which so greatly influence our thinking and decisions. We are overly passive. Politicians sell themselves out prior to elections to win support; after elections they make political payoffs with job appointments, placing in key influential positions persons whose views on moral issues in no way reflect their own. In this and other ways we compromise, and the end result is a selling out to that which is contrary to what we know deep in our hearts is really right. The dilemma is real but self-imposed.

If we do not recognize as Christians that we are engaged in a battle, and if we are not going to put on the whole armor of God, we are not going to be prepared for the kind of spiritual warfare the Bible tells us we will have to wage (*see* Ephesians 6:11–17).

The day of the comfortable Christian is over. As distasteful as it is to say that, it must be said. We are living in a sin-ridden world. Are you willing to stand with those who not only claim to believe the Bible, but are willing to follow up with dynamic Christian application, and are willing to speak up and proclaim the truth?

The Book of James says that a bare faith without a corresponding life is useless and dead. Our faith is to be implemented by our deeds. This means that in the practical outworking of our faith we seize every opportunity to speak up for the Lord, and we use the means available to us to bring about change. We must not simply condemn, but we must be ready for involvement as we seek to help reaffirm those who are willing to give up their sinful bents.

Are we willing to say to the homosexual, ". . . a man's temptation is due to the pull of his own inward desires, which greatly attract him. It is his own desire which conceives and gives birth to sin. And sin when full grown produces death—make no mistake about that, brothers of mine! . . . Have done, then, with impurity and every other evil which overflows into the lives of others, and humbly accept the message . . . which can save your souls'' (James 1:14–16, 19, 21 PHILLIPS).

The hour is serious. Time is short. I believe with all my heart that the Lord is coming soon. I have at times been filled with a supernatural joy as I contemplate the fact that one of these days God is going to release us from the heartaches and pain we experience here. I look forward to that day. And that explains why I am willing to expend myself beyond what I know I need to do. I am compelled of God. I know the urgency. But even in that urgency, knowing the hour is near, I am also learning patience and not to run ahead of God. Each thing has its own time.

The year 1977 was a time of learning to wait upon God. The year 1978—even while writing this—has been a time of further schooling as the Holy Spirit continues to show me the things I need to learn. There have been many lessons He has needed to teach me and is continuing to teach me. One of the things He has impressed upon me is the willingness to be expendable and available to Him. This means I must spare no effort in reaching out with the truth. If the time on earth for Christians is short, it is short for the unsaved too.

Repeatedly I am asked, ''Anita, aren't you fearful for your life?'' No, I am not afraid under *any* circumstance. I have more fear of being made a fool in a courtroom, or at a press conference, or disgracing the Lord as far as my ignorance of the law or other questions that might be thrown at me, but I do not fear for myself, nor do I care anymore what is said about me personally. They can call me a ''rednecked bigot,'' or whatever other disgraceful names they can dredge up, but it's all right. It is the Lord I do not want to bring reproach upon. No, death threats do not bother me. The Apostle said to be absent from the body is to be present with the Lord (*see* 2 Corinthians 5:8).

I have said on several occasions that all the money in the world couldn't pay me and our family for what we've come through.

One threat of death would be enough to make anyone quit, but God has promised to protect us, and no one can touch us unless God allows it for His purpose. He has shown Himself mighty and merciful on our behalf, and we are trusting in Him. There are hundreds who have expressed concern about threats made upon my life. I really have no fear. I believe I could walk through a crowd of jeering, angry homosexual protestors and that I would be unharmed. I have confidence to believe that God would surround me with protecting unseen angelic forces.

Things of spiritual value are of first importance. The day of being comfortable Christians is over for Bob and me.

4
The Chasm

> Sexual immorality is a state of mind, like criminality,
> where justification of the act is in the mind of the doer.
> ALEX SCOROFF, quoted in the Cocoa, Florida, *Today*

Who brought the subject of homosexuality into the limelight? Was it my wife?

Has she ever said, "The homosexual is not worthy to be *my* neighbor"? Either by actual statement or implication, has my wife said or done that? Amazingly, you can obtain "Christian" books today that attribute that statement and others of a like defamatory nature to Anita.

Such thinly disguised attempts to discredit Anita and make her out to be a bigoted self-righteous, right-wing fanatic are more damaging to the cause of Christianity than they are, in fact, to my wife personally. There will be those, however, who will swallow this verbiage, repeat it to others, and defame far more than the name of Anita Bryant. The Bible carries severe warnings of God's contempt of those who spread falsehood. God's displeasure is shown through His Old Testament prophets who unflinchingly stood up and declared warnings from the Lord. Malachi was one such prophet. Those who write Christian books and profess to be knowledgeable about the Word of God fall into a similar category with the priests about whom Malachi spoke.

"Priests' lips should flow with the knowledge of God so the people will learn God's laws. The priests are the messengers of the Lord of Hosts, and men should come to them for guidance. But not to you! For you have left God's paths. Your 'guidance' has caused many to stumble in sin. You have distorted the covenant of Levi, and made it into a grotesque parody," says the Lord of Hosts.

Malachi 2:7, 8 LB

The prophet asked a question that we, as Christians, should be asking ourselves before we open our mouths to speak profanely against each other. Malachi said, "Have we not all one father? hath not one God created us? why do we deal treacherously every man against his brother . . . ?" (2:10).

I feel compelled to ask additional questions. Has Anita looked down upon the homosexual as being less than fully human? Has she robbed them of respect, opportunity, and even life itself? Indeed, has either one of us set out to ostracize them? Have we assaulted their dignity, torn down their pride? Have we been unwilling to listen to them? Have we refused to converse with them? Have we failed in trying to understand them? When we say we love them, are we being hypocrites mouthing that out of one corner of our mouths and then saying or doing something else when the media's backs are turned? And who is judging whom when the indictment is leveled that my wife brandishes Bible texts like weapons? And who is failing both by word and deed? All these and many more ugly untruths have been spread about my wife both in writing and speaking by not only those who are militant homosexuals, but worse, by those who maintain that they are compassionate Christians.

Who is harassing whom? Who is intimidating whom? Who is advocating boycotts against Anita personally and against the states which have failed to ratify the ERA?

Statements, attributed to Anita, have come from the biased, wordly secular media—statements that have been so twisted and contorted that they bear no resemblence whatsoever to what Anita has in fact actually said. Yet such books and individuals report these statements as fact, going so far as to say that she has "threatened" homosexuals. They also contort statements by such well-known and respected ministers as Jerry Falwell. And the much-reported bumper sticker KILL A QUEER FOR CHRIST has been attributed to my wife but we, in fact, have *never* seen one in our lives!

Such authors continue to spread the false rumor that we are out to take away the civil rights of homosexuals, equating homosexuals with legitimate minority groups. They report what my wife says as "abusive language."

Turning to the founder of psychoanalysis, Sigmund Freud, such writers quote him as the final authority. (Freud has been identified as a humanist who developed his total sexual mythology on a radical atheistic basis.) Books by those who claim to be Christians, who insist that Freud, not the Word of God, is right and to be followed and believed, now abound, with such writers calling into question *our* Christian beliefs based solidly on Scripture.

Anita has consistently called attention to 1 Corinthians 6:9–11 which says that homosexuals can overcome their abnormal sexual appetite and bring it under the control of Christ. It is a demonstration of the power of the Holy Spirit.

Know ye not that the unrighteous shall not inherit the kingdom of God? Be not deceived: neither fornicators, nor idolaters, nor adulterers, nor effeminate, nor abusers of themselves with mankind, Nor thieves, nor covetous, nor drunkards, nor revilers, nor extortioners, shall inherit the kingdom of God. And such were some of you: but ye are washed, but ye are sanctified, but ye are justified in the name of the Lord Jesus, and by the Spirit of our God.

Liberal writers call this "simplistic." These same writers believe the Bible to be "culturally conditioned, and not everything therein is eternally authoritative." Such as these claim the Apostle Paul "did not understand that true homosexuals have a *natural* inclination toward members of their own sex." They point to Romans 14:14 which says, ". . . nothing is impure in itself . . ." (NEB), and that apparently, according to them, wipes out other references to the act of homosexuality as being an "abomination to God."

"Gay" evangelicals and their sympathizers contend that if homosexual practice is intended to express love as part of an "ongoing, permanent relationship, rather than lust, it is morally good" (Richard Quebedeaux, *The Worldly Evangelicals*).

Those subscribing to this so-called "new morality," which is as old as sin itself, are maintaining that the Apostle Paul really did not mean what we as evangelical believers have long thought he meant. This emergence of a "new morality," is based on reason, experience, and the situation in question, and "love is really the only absolute ethical norm."

Clearly, a chasm of more immense proportions than the average churchgoing Christian knows exists between what is now being called "left" evangelicals and "right" evangelicals. Anita has been branded by the "left" evangelicals, and while they maintain that *she* has made the homosexual a scapegoat and has imposed upon them social ostracism, there is no admission on their part that the homosexual community has done anything wrong nor that they have made Anita *their* scapegoat.

The homosexual community itself, however, states that it coauthored the controversial Dade County Human Rights Law with an up-front appeal to the politicians, much behind-the-scenes lobbying, and a persevering process which began with our local Fair Housing and Appeals Board. They brazenly say they created the force necessary for the full consciousness development of their goals. "We created Anita Bryant," they proclaim in their newsletters.

The press has fallen for their rhetoric. "Left" evangelicals, who have for the most part abandoned traditional Christian views, have fallen in step with the liberal press and the homosexual community. There is no recognition that the Bible is transcultural and that its truth is as relevant for society today as it was in times past. What does their line of reasoning do with such verses as Hebrews 13:8? "Jesus Christ the same yesterday, and to day, and for ever."

I am sickened as I read things which are being written now by those who claim to be "enlightened Christians," books and articles which will be instrumental in shaping the thinking of impressionable young people, and other more mature Christians who, unfortunately, often are easily swayed and are not grounded sufficiently in the Bible to realize what is happening.

We are living in the days described by Jesus who said that some of the very elect shall even be led astray (*see* Matthew 24:24). Jesus also told us that unless these days are shortened, all mankind will perish. But He has given His promise that these days will be shortened for the sake of God's chosen people.

Christian psychiatrist Dr. James Parsons and Christian psychologist Dr. George Rekers are representative of those whose leanings are in accord with the view taken by Anita and me. Doctor Kenneth Gangel, author of the important new book *The Gospel and the Gay,* Jerry Kirk, author of the book *The Homosexual Crisis in the Mainline Church,* and others' views reflect clear, compassionate, and balanced guidance that holds to biblical teachings.

Doctor Rekers attended the two-day brainstorming session at our home and gave us valuable insights which are helping to shape the future direction the Anita Bryant Ministries and Protect America's Children will go.

Writers with a humanist view would welcome practicing homosexuals into every area of church life, including ordination, without requiring obedience to the revealed, will of God, that is giving up one's participation in homosexual relationships. The Bible talks of this kind of conduct:

For certain persons have crept in unnoticed . . . ungodly
persons who turn the grace of our God into licentiousness
and deny our only Master and Lord, Jesus Christ . . . Just as
Sodom and Gomorrah and the cities around them, since they
in the same way as these indulged in gross immorality and
went after strange flesh, are exhibited as an example . . . .
these men, also by dreaming, defile the flesh, and reject authority . . . . Woe to them! . . . These men . . . caring for
themselves . . . doubly dead . . . . wild waves of the sea,
casting up their own shame like foam; wandering stars, for
whom the black darkness has been reserved forever . . . .
following after their own lusts . . . . But you, beloved,
ought to remember the words that were spoken beforehand
by the apostles of our Lord Jesus Christ, that they were
saying to you, "In the last time there shall be mockers, following after their own ungodly lusts." These are the ones
who cause divisions, worldly-minded, devoid of the Spirit.

Jude 4, 7, 8, 11–13, 16–19 NAS

That book from the Bible is a warning of history to the ungodly,
and it is a call to obedient Christians to "contend earnestly for the
faith" (*see* v. 3 NAS). Anita takes literally the admonition in this
book which tells the Christian to "have mercy on some, who are
doubting; save others, snatching them out of the fire; and on some
have mercy with fear . . ." (vv. 22, 23 NAS).

As I see the things that happen on a daily basis, I find it necessary to remind Anita and myself that we must not look at this as a
bleak picture, but regard it as a positive thing that God has used,
and that she has been a sort of catalyst.

Madalyn O'Hair became known as a "Missionary for
Atheism," when she won a Supreme Court case in 1963 that
banned compulsory prayer from public schools. Out to stop what
she called "the official intrusion of religion," the woman has been
relentless in her pursuit of what she considers her cause.

Anita, on the other hand, did not seek publicity nor set out initially on any kind of national crusade. In a typical example of American democracy at work, the homosexuals lost and the parents and concerned citizens of Miami won the Dade County referendum vote. Regardless of conflicting claims, the whole issue was really settled by that vote, notwithstanding our involvement. The matter should have rested there—but it hasn't. The militant homosexuals singled out Anita as their target for a continuing campaign. Regardless where we went in the days following the Dade County vote, we were picketed, followed, and the press would not let us alone. Newspaper headlines screamed out in advance of our arrival such things as: IN COMES ANITA HEAVILY GUARDED. The truth was we never came in with our own guards to any city (local security was provided because the cities did not wish to be held responsible for what could happen to Anita). As we recognized what was happening, Anita and I had to come to the conclusion that she had no choice but to keep on paying the price in her efforts to help the godly and concerned people in this nation.

Someone sent us a letter in which he urged: "Stay faithful to the faith, faithful to the fight, faithful to the finish. Keep your eyes on the Lord, keep your heart in the Word, keep your knees on the prayer bench—and you'll never have any trouble standing on your feet."

I'm proud of Anita and the way she manages to keep on standing on her feet. The secret, if you can call it that, to how she manages to do this and still be a good wife and a tremendous mother to our four children, lies in the fact that Anita allows nothing to spoil her relationship with God. I have heard her on her knees thanking God for the viciousness of the media's continued attacks and the demonstrations by "gays" and their supporters.

Anita believes, and so do I, that if God puts His hand upon us for a particular task, we must not frustrate His plan. We must be available and willing to be used.

I am really sorry when I read statements by people such as Dr. Rollo May, psychoanalyst and psychotherapist, as well as an author, who says Anita has been leading a "campaign of dogma against other people's jobs," and that he is urging people to give up their "old ideas of God."

I am sorry when I read books such as *Is the Homosexual My Neighbor?* by authors Letha Scanzoni and Virgina Ramey Mollenkott who distort the much-loved and familiar Bible story about the Good Samaritan (*see* Luke 10:25–37). They state that if that story were reenacted in the setting of today, the man who fell among thieves would be the equivalent of practicing homosexuals, and people who hold the view of biblical morality, like Anita and myself, would be the priest and Levite who passed by without offering compassion and help.

I am sorry that at press conferences reporters can no longer report objectively, and that their stories are biased, reflecting their own prejudices and disdain of godliness and Christianity. They find it necessary to heap scorn upon Anita, warping her words viciously, trying to bait her, and when they are unsuccessful, end up browbeating her. Journalism's traditional purpose has been to inform and enlighten; we have seen very little of that in comparison to the amount of flak Anita has had to take.

I am truly sorry for the verbal bludgeoning that my wife has endured. Even if she had not been my wife, as one Christian looking upon what has been allowed in the media, I could not have remained silent.

At times the weight of sorrow has been almost overwhelming. At such times, we buoy each other up by reminding ourselves that Jesus carried a crushing weight—the sinfulness of the world—all the way to the cruel cross for us. That is a historical fact as well as coming straight from the Bible—the same Bible which says sin is sin, including the sin of homosexuality.

The sorrow I feel compels me to say that it is not the magnitude of sin that keeps a man from God, it's *sin*. Jesus said: "He that heareth you heareth me; and he that despiseth you despiseth me; and he that despiseth me despiseth him that sent me" (Luke 10:16).

5
Out of the Closet

> But thou, when thou prayest, enter into thy closet, and
> when thou hast shut thy door, pray to thy Father
> which is in secret; and thy Father which seeth in secret
> shall reward thee openly.
>
> Matthew 6:6

One day it dawned on me—I was "out of the closet," too. The
homosexual community talks of "coming out of the closet," and
every time I read or heard that phrase, something inside me
reached out in understanding and my heart hurt for them. When
you make a deliberate choice and take a stand, it requires courage, and so in a sense I could identify with what the homosexual
was saying. Once I had overcome my apathy I could not go back
to the position of noninvolvement as before.

A reporter for the *Wittenburg Door* asked some penetrating
questions. Framing answers to his questions helped to crystallize
my thoughts. I was glad for the opportunity it and other such
objective interviews presented me to confront my own deep inner
feelings. When he asked, "Are you sick of this issue? Do you
wish you could go back to the way it was?" I found myself reply-
ing with complete candor. I told him, "I know too much now and
for that I'm grateful. In a sense I'm 'out of the closet,' too, and I
have no intention of going back."

I have often told Bob that if I didn't have the Lord to talk to,
I'd be in an asylum. Communication with many friends was cut

51

off, not by choice necessarily on their part, but because association with me at this juncture in their lives would make it difficult for them in their professional pursuits. The irony of this has been that even those holding the same deep inner convictions have dared not come "out of the closet." Their careers would be in jeopardy; ministries would be endangered and suffer, and, as Bob says, "They'd go right down even as your stature in the entertainment industry has been virtually destroyed." This in a country that prides itself on its freedoms! It is almost inconceivable that this could happen in America.

Difficult as this was to accept, nevertheless I asked God to enlarge my capacity to understand. When the *Wittenburg Door* reporter asked if we were disappointed that other religious leaders didn't support us, and did we feel alone, I had to answer with a truthful *yes*. I hastened to add, however, that there were those who were willing to stick out their necks, as it were, and who openly let it be known that they were standing with us. I pointed out that we have continued to receive an incredible amount of mail. God has His faithful people out there who have given unstintingly of their love—people like Danny and Jolene Urschel and Rufus and Norma Schackelford. We know we are not altogether alone.

The media's first tactic, like the militant homosexuals themselves, was to attack us personally, to start digging to try to find ways to discredit us. One thing in particular the press did was to try to cast a shadow over our financial situation. Reports cropped up all across the country as to the status of our finances. Then, later, we were made to appear as opportunists preying on a gullible public and using our organization as a means to make money to pay for our life-style.

We remained silent through such attacks. Even today at press conferences, inevitably one of the reporters will ask a question relating to our finances. Bob has some interesting thoughts on this subject which he'll relate in chapter eight.

Readers and supporters of Protect America's Children, however, have a right to know that everything that comes into the organization is used solely to support the efforts of citizens of cities such as Saint Paul and Wichita, to defray the office expenses, and to help set up a legal task force to give specialized help where needed. As this book is being written, plans are in the embryonic stage to start a counseling ministry to homosexuals who want a way out of their sad, not gay, life-style. This will be set up through Anita Bryant Ministries.

It has been a humbling experience for me as an entertainer to admit that if we were going to help other cities, we would have to rely on financial help to meet the many needs. "Bob, I can't do that," I argued. Bob is a stable force in our family and the practical one. He's also the one who has to remind me constantly that we have to pay our bills. He reminded me gently but firmly that my days as an entertainer apparently were drawing to a close and that we were left with no choice. Subdued, I agreed with his assessment of the situation. "God is behind this entire organization, Bob," I said, "and that settles it." With that I swallowed my pride. No one can know how much I wish it were possible that from my earnings as an entertainer I could pick up the tab for all the expenses involved in running an organization such as Protect America's Children. Those earnings have, of course, now been virtually cut off, as far as secular bookings are concerned.

There has been continuing speculation that my motives in getting involved in the Dade County campaign were politically inspired. Despite my repeated disclaimers, many politicians in particular, citizens in general, and the militant homosexuals have predicted that I would ride the Miami referendum into an elected office in the state of Florida. The suggestion is so alien to my intentions that we have refused to even bother with a counter-reply. We've been accused of "hopscotching around the country, talking up our cause." It's been said that we are "puppets" of a right-wing-establishment conspiracy and we have rooms full of think tanks, computers, and men figuring out "battle plans."

The truth is that we've had mainly housewives and mothers

opening mail, answering letters and phones, and Bob sitting behind a desk in a not-very-fancy office building. More recently, we've had to enlist the help of Ed Rowe to serve in the capacity of an executive director. This, however, is the extent of our work. With limited help, limited funds, and the prayers and hard work of dedicated people, we are committed to whatever God calls us to do.

It was interesting that while show-business personalities were entertaining at a "Celebration for Human Rights" rally in the Hollywood Bowl and *Newsweek* magazine predicted that other such rallies would be staged "to counteract the abundant publicity that Bryant is likely to get from her book," my publisher and I were canceling what few events we did have lined up for the usual promotion which had always accompanied the publication of my books. Such cancellation became necessary, seeming the better part of wisdom to spare booksellers and department stores the harrassment of heckling homosexual demonstrators.

In contrast, however, the media reported the tours Rod McKuen was on to promote one of his books. McKuen boasted that his writing was hitting at Billy Graham and me. Interestingly, so-called "straight" society and people like Bob and I were *not* out there protesting, picketing, and demonstrating in front of stores where *he* was appearing. Frankly, we wouldn't waste our time.

A friend wrote to tell of the Christian bookstore in the city where she lived and what had happened to a shipment of *The Anita Bryant Story*. Someone had defaced the entire supply! The woman wrote: "When I heard that, I cried . . . . Then I called other religious bookstores in the city and warned them. The bookstore owners were of one accord—they'd have to pray and trust the Lord to protect their supply of the book." The woman ended her letter by stating, "I don't think I've ever prayed for books before, but in this day and age there's a first time for all kinds of things that need our prayer . . . ."

When I read that, I thought of Ezekiel 22:30:

And I sought for a man among them, that should make up the hedge, and stand in the gap before me for the land, that I should not destroy it . . . .

Paul E. Billheimer in his book *Destined for the Throne* asks: "Has it ever occurred to you that the design in the divine economy is a fantastically puzzling mystery?"

I've often thought of that—does God really need our prayers? David in Psalm 8 said what has on occasion been in my thoughts: "I cannot understand how you can bother with mere puny man, to pay any attention to him!" (v. 4 LB).

Billheimer points out that it was in a time of national apostasy that God said what He did to Ezekiel, as He sought to avoid exercising just and deserved punishment upon that nation. Because He is a God of justice and love, He longs to spare apostate people. I do not pretend to understand the supreme Judge of this universe and this seemingly baffling mystery of our importance in God's scheme of things, and therefore the need for us to pray. We are not only exhorted to pray, but we are commanded to do so and God, furthermore, has promised to answer. Billheimer says prayer is on-the-job training for sovereignty, an apprenticeship, if you will, for co-reigning with Christ over His universal empire. "By our failure to pray we are frustrating God's high purpose in the ages. We are robbing the world of God's best plan for it and we are limiting our rank in eternity."

People often say, "But what can we do, Anita, to help at this crucial time in our nation's history? What can we do to protect our own and other people's children?" You can, among other things, write to us. Share your concerns and ideas. Every piece of mail that comes into our offices is given careful attention. We are listening to what you are telling us. You are helping to provide the direction we need. (See the last chapter for our correct mailing address and plans for the future.)

Increasingly I am convinced that the thing that will have the greatest impact in bringing about change is *prayer.* Our good friends Bill and Vonette Bright of Campus Crusade for Christ International have seen demonstrated what happens when God's people rally and pray. They state: "Your prayers can help change the world." The Great Commission Prayer Crusade, launched by Vonette Bright as coordinator and Mrs. Billy Graham as honorary chairperson in February 1972, has brought about a dynamic prayer movement that encompasses Christian men and women of all ages and interests. (Write to Campus Crusade for Christ International, Arrowhead Springs, San Bernardino, CA, 92414, and ask for their Strategy Manuals Volumes 1 and 2 on prayer.) As Christians who are concerned, we need to come out of our "prayer closets" ready to identify with what's happening. We need to be available to respond where action is required and work needs to be done. We must show our compassion for homosexuals in caring and tangible ways. We must put to rest the charge that we are "homophobiacs" (guilty of fearing and rejecting homosexuals as people), an undeserved charge for the majority of Christians I know. That is a term that has been bandied about by homosexuals and liberal Christians alike. We have been accused of gross lovelessness when, in truth, the only thing that could keep anyone going in a situation such as we've confronted is our great love and concern for those who are tampering with the Bible and for those who are homosexual supporters and practicing homosexuals themselves.

How much we need the power that comes through prayer! S. D. Gordon said, "The greatest thing anyone can do for God and for man is to pray." That same man said, "You can do more than pray *after* you have prayed, but you cannot do more than pray *until* you have prayed."

Because we are misunderstood, because our words and answers to reporters and interviewers who approach the subject from an entirely different position is so different, our greatest single resource is prayer. How many times have I tried in my own strength to get across a point and failed! Proof of that is the seemingly contradictory statements I have made on some occasions while being interviewed. It's been very difficult; many times I've felt like I was being baited and backed into a corner. My replies have not always come off sounding as I mean them. I've taken comfort in Ephesians 6:13, 18, 19:

> . . . having done all, to stand . . . . Praying always with all prayer and supplication in the Spirit, and watching thereunto with all perseverance and supplication for all saints; And for me, that utterance may be given unto me, that I may open my mouth boldly, to make known the mystery of the gospel.

Bob and I recognize our fallibility. We've been pounced on pretty hard because of it. We're going to make some more mistakes, not deliberately, but because we are human. But we are going to continue to stand and trust God to take our blundering efforts, combined with our prayers, and the prayers of God's people, to bring about good.

Jerry Kirk in his book *The Homosexual Crisis in the Mainline Church* says there are three keys to helping homosexuals, "homophobiacs," or other sinners:

1. Make sure they are aware that you know *you* are as big a sinner as they. (And don't fake it. If you don't believe you're as big a sinner, how come?)
2. Accept them as friends—real friends.
3. Call them to a godly life.

Here is a respected pastor in the Presbyterian church saying what I have been advocating from the word *go*. Yet I am accused of being "homophobiac." It doesn't add up. Not only have I been saying this, I have been demonstrating it.

Jim Bishop in the *Miami Herald* (January 29, 1978) wrote a strong open letter to me in which he questioned: "Are you saving children?" He concluded by accusing me of being up to my nostrils in obscure psychology, and then stated: "I would like you to bring one child to me and let him explain how you saved him. Just one. I'll be happy to publicize the story."

The *Herald* offered equal space for rebuttal. It was easy. We had many letters from which to choose. We chose six, representative as they were of the many who write revealing how they have been set free of homosexuality by the power and love of Jesus Christ. It is not by anything we have done other than to speak boldly calling homosexuals to repent and live a godly life, but because of God's answer to prayers. Anita Bryant hasn't "saved" them, Jesus Christ has!

These are some of the excerpts printed in the *Miami Herald*:

- I am gay. I want to change. I long for marriage and children, all you are blessed with. I believe you are meant to fight this battle. I support you in my daily prayers.

- Jesus came into my life about a year and a half ago. I was gay. Thank you, Anita, for coming out against the homosexual world. The only true gay liberation is believing that Jesus is Lord, and in repentance from the abominable sin of homosexuality.

- I am a 27-year-old man who has been set free of homosexuality by the power and love of Jesus Christ.

  I know what a false life, a lonely life that gay life is. All I ever wanted was true love. I never found it through lovers, but I found it when I allowed Jesus to be Lord of my life.

  Because of your ministry, there are going to be thousands set free. For every stand you take, you have the prayers in abundance of Christians everywhere.

- Dec. 25 was a turning point in my life, as the Holy Spirit directed me to stand before a packed church and give my testimony of how Jesus had set me free of being a homosexual.

I couldn't before understand how you could profess to be a Christian and want to deny homosexuals their rights, nor could I understand how you could stand there and say you loved them.

I understand now, and I thank God every day for such a wonderful person like you. Because you did love us, you put yourself on the line and condemned the terrible lifestyle that goes along with that way!

6

Pie in the Face and Other Less Publicized Things

> O my God, save me from my enemies. Protect me from these who have come to destroy me. Preserve me . . . . They lurk in ambush for my life. Strong men are out there waiting. And not, O Lord, because I've done them wrong.
>
> PSALMS 59:1–3 LB

"Homosexual organizations such as the Gay Activist Alliance have been unswerving in their dedication to nonviolent methods," so states some of the homosexual supporters' literature. The implication is that those who stand in opposition to flaunting homosexuals are vicious and that *we* are harrassing the homosexual. Nothing could be further from the truth. Have you seen my wife in *any* sort of vicious demonstration against homosexuals?

In contrast, let me fill you in on a few never-publicized details which Anita and Protect America's Children office workers have encountered. One day we opened up our post-office box, and there was an unmistakable odor. The question was, where? Some things are not caught in the process of opening the large volume of mail which we receive. How would you have liked to be the person opening the box that contained someone else's excrement? We have had dead cockroaches and rotten oranges sent to us. Some have shown their dislike for our literature by using it for toilet paper and sending it back to us.

How would you men feel if you opened a letter, and there was a photo of your wife's head superimposed on some other female nude body in the most lewd and shocking sexual act you can imagine? I ask you, male reader, husband, how would *you* feel about that? The naked pictures of homosexuals doing "their thing" has been nauseating. Other pornographic materials sent us have filled box after box of trash.

If you are really opposed to Anita Bryant, you can buy toilet paper with her face printed continuously on each sheet. Its advertisement reads: WIPE THAT SMILE (crossed out and SMIRK inserted above) OFF ANITA (STANDARD-SIZE ROLL OF TP WITH HER LOVELY FACE PRINTED CONTINUOUSLY ON ENTIRE ROLL . . . . YOU CAN'T MISS!) That may be nonviolent, but it's hardly decent, loving, or neighborly. It is not the type of thing the biblical Good Samaritan would have done.

Nonviolent? What do you call cutting the ropes on a tent where 3,500 people are gathered to hear and see Cecil Todd and Anita in a Revive America Campaign?

And my wife's being forced because of bomb threats and demonstrations to flee New York after canceling a news conference and events planned to coincide with the publication of *The Anita Bryant Story,* would you call that nonviolent?

What kind of loving neighborliness is it on the part of the homosexual and homosexual supporters who print in their college paper that they are "appalled and disgusted because the University will soon be disgraced by the appearance of Anita Bryant"? Another sheet distributed in a city where she was due to appear stated: "The voice of bigotry and hate is to appear in ———."

It's fine for entertainers and stars to appear on national TV condemning my wife and satirizing her in the most uncomplimentary ways imaginable; it's fine for the Johnny Carsons, the Carol Burnetts, and others to make her the brunt of their sick jokes; but let word get out that Anita is to appear on a TV program, and the threats of bombings and disruptions cause the network to cancel the show. Or the Federal Communications Commission is contacted by the homosexuals who insist that the "fairness doctrine" be invoked at once to allow homosexuals to appear on TV to counter criticism of their life-style. They insist on equal time and/or space in the media when Anita is performing as an entertainer, not there to talk about the homosexual issue.

Mike Douglas has had Anita on his show as a performer many times. When *The Anita Bryant Story* came out, the publisher wanted her on the show to promote the book, to sing, and to do what she's done before on the program, but they couldn't put her on unless they had a member of the "gay" community there also. I have watched *The Mike Douglas Show*, *The Dinah Shore Show*, and others, and they have featured Ed Asner, Jane Fonda, Shirley MacLaine, Florence Henderson, and other actors and actresses who are outspoken homosexual supporters, but Anita is not allowed to come on as an entertainer as she has in the past.

What hurts is that Anita is being denied rights as an American. Other entertainers can operate in an activist role on the liberal side—pro-ERA, pro-abortion, pro-gay-rights—and they are able to work and appear unhasseled, with no conservatives picketing or demonstrating. Among other things, it shows the hypocrisy of the civil libertarians in not coming to Anita's defense of her right to work and her right of free speech. Anita has been punished severely, her name dragged through the mud, and her stature as an entertainer and as a person demeaned without cause.

If the tables had been turned, and Anita Bryant were a Shirley MacLaine, and the issue were Shirley MacLaine against the conservatives in Dade County, Florida, what would have happened? Would the conservatives have picketed? Would they have hasseled Shirley as an entertainer? No, they would not. What if on June 7, 1977, it had been reported that the Anita Bryant forces had lost? Would we have started boycotts against the programs or products represented by Ed Asner, for instance?

Many performers have come out against Anita. We consider it their right as Americans. I can still watch those people perform and in the proper setting and format, and I can still appreciate their talent. But they cannot do the same. When they hate, they hate the person; whereas we can hate the sin and love the person. The liberals' hatred is not partial, but total. When they hated Anita for her stand, they hated every aspect of her life—her children, her husband, her as a performer. If it was said that Anita had no talent, was a bad performer, or did commercials badly—and was true—I could live with that. But for the homosexual community and their supporters to come at her the way they have, has been without excuse. When you analyze their vindictiveness and what has been done, it is plain to see the evil forces that are at work.

I have asked myself what would make me hate somebody as much as the liberals hate Anita, and I can think of nothing. If somebody blasphemes my Lord, there is anger, but it is righteous indignation, and I would not go on a campaign after them. The Bible tells me to pray for such as these, and that's what we have been doing.

A sustaining knowledge has been that Jesus forewarned that we could expect hatred from the world. "If the world hate you, ye know that it hated me before it hated you" (John 15:18).

Across the nation hatred for Anita is shown by buying T-shirts that say ANITA BRYANT SUCKS ORANGES or PUT THE SQUEEZE ON ANITA BRYANT. There is a "Stick It to Anita Bryant Boutique," in New York that sells books titled *The Bible According to St. Anita,* and *Anita Bryant's Jokes for My John.* They also do a brisk business in T-shirts which read, ANITA BRYANT FONDLES ORANGES. A place in Phoenix advertises windbreaker cushions that make a foul noise when sat upon, and read, ANITA'S LAST BREATH. They suggest you buy one and "sit on Anita's face (again and again and again)."

We have seen stacks of material of this nature—a photo of a donkey with Anita's picture on the animal's rear, a billboard that reads ANITA FOR FÜHRER, and an advertisement offering four sharp darts and a two-sided board with Anita's picture and the label STICK ANITA AS MUCH AS YOU WANT.

The clincher of "nonviolent" acts—which certain writers, homosexuals, and homosexual supporters would have us believe are just that—came in Des Moines when Anita was unceremoniously plastered with a banana-cream pie, bull's-eye (as one writer put it), in her face. I responded to that attack on my wife with what I believe was wisdom the Lord provided at the time I needed it most. It all happened in a split second. I looked up and saw the man's hand go by with the pie (which at the time, I couldn't recognize as such). The first reaction was forgiveness. Almost at the same time as I saw the man's hand, I saw cameras moving away from Anita. In other words, they got the shot they wanted of Anita getting the pie. Now they were moving away from Anita, and I watched that movement closely. The cameras were focused on this individual standing there with his arms raised in an "I give up" position. In that instant I realized that the opposition's goal was to see Anita's Christian husband jump over the table and belt this guy.

The pictures and the TV would have shown this "poor, helpless individual, standing with his hands up in the air, and the Christian husband, who was supposed to be forgiving, belting him." That would have been the story. The story would *not* have been that Anita got the pie, but that Anita's husband was hitting the "poor guy." At that point—remember, it all happened in a split second—the Lord provided the wisdom, and I said to myself, "I'm not going to give the media and the 'gays' that opportunity."

Anita was in a momentary state of shock. Deep down inside she was probably instantaneously angry at me for *not* belting the guy—and I can accept that—but we both realized that without question I did the right thing. I am human, however, and this was the woman I love being treated with such contempt. Humanly speaking, I wanted to jump over the table and give him what he had coming.

I asked Anita to pray for the man, and I ordered that no one touch him. In the true tradition of great entertainers, my wife prayed, kept her cool, and afterward said, "At least it's a fruit pie."

The fellow joined three companions outside the door where the press conference was being held. The others had pies in their hands too. The plan was, it appeared, that after I'd belted the guy and the security guards had rushed Anita out, they'd pelt her again with more pies. But that's *not* the way it happened because we foiled their plans.

A matter of minutes went by. Anita was cleaning up. I looked out the window, and there were reporters standing in a circle around some people, so I walked out to check on what was happening. I stood several yards away and observed the four homosexuals in the process of having a press conference. It was "show and tell time" for them.

The three remaining pies were out of the boxes, and they were telling everyone in great detail how they'd planned the attack, the route they'd used, and how one had managed to infiltrate the press conference by posing as a reporter. That I could not tolerate! One was standing with a pie, showing how it had been smashed squarely in Anita's face. I walked calmly over to him, put my hand under his, raised his hand up into his face, and wiped the pie over his face. At that point everyone started throwing pies at each other. I said to the man, "How does it feel?"

They started screaming at me, saying, "You forgave us inside; you're a hypocrite . . . ." I walked away and while cleaning myself up, two reporters from Des Moines came over and started asking me about the incident outside. "You had forgiven them inside. Why did you do that?"

I explained that they were exploiting it outside by having the separate press conference. As far as we were concerned inside, the incident was over and done with. When I came out and saw what they were doing and listened to them, I gave them exactly what they deserved. I am very human with human frailties. I asked the reporters, "How would *you* have reacted if it had been your wife?'' At that point it hit them what had taken place. They told me in no uncertain terms what they would have done physically to anyone who did such a thing to their wives. That stopped their line of questioning.

I have been severely criticized, particularly by some of the "left" evangelicals in their magazines. I was wrong but carry no guilt about that incident. What happened inside in front of the TV cameras was a spontaneous reaction, but God directed, of that I am confident. What happened outside was not in contradiction. I believe the Lord allowed me to respond as a husband in another entirely unrehearsed spontaneous reaction.

The story that surfaced later revealed that the four homosexuals had made a special trip from Minneapolis to Des Moines. The assailant was asked what he thought his stunt had gained. ''We have another bigot with a sticky face,'' was his reply. Anita and I chose *not* to press charges.

The attack was not so much on Anita personally. When the pie was thrown in Anita's face, all Christians got that pie. When they attack Anita, they are attacking the church—the Body of Christ and His people.

But I take this means—this book—to ask God-fearing Americans and Christians to continue to intercede in prayer for my wife. That pie could have been a gun, or some other weapon. Have you ever thought about that? Pray for God's continued protection for the woman who is my wife and the mother of our children.

7
Spiritual Warfare in the Worldly Arena

> We all stand in a higher court than the one where we
> are judged by our fellowman. It is the verdict of that
> higher court that really counts. The secret to great
> living is to have a clear conscience no matter what the
> judgment of our detractors may be.
>
> ERNEST A. FITZGERALD quoted in *Pace* magazine

Bob feels stronger than I do about these insults and things that
happen to me. Ken Kelly, writing in *Playboy* magazine (more
about that in another chapter), says Bob is the "moving target for
the slings and arrows of Anita's abuse," and, in a sense, that's
sometimes the case. All that's happened to us has been hard on
our relationship; on the other hand, it's drawn us closer. I can't
explain it; neither can Bob. Because of the unbelievable stresses
we experience, our nerves are sometimes frayed. We each realize
that if we have to vent our emotions, it is best to vent them on
each other.

When the pie landed in my face, I did go into a momentary state
of shock. I was waiting for Bob to leap over and punch the guy.
That was my human nature responding. Instead, Bob took my
hand. My eyes were covered with pie, and I couldn't see anything. Moments before, the same guy had been questioning me,
posing as a reporter. The tip-off that he himself was possibly
homosexual came when he said to me, "Miss Bryant, what are

some of *your* sins?'' We'd been talking about the need for sinners
to repent and ask God's forgiveness for their sins.

I answered him by stating that I didn't care to flaunt my sins
and, as a matter of fact, I repent of them to God. I said, ''I'm so
ashamed of my sinfulness that I don't care to flaunt it.''

And then it happened! Smack! Pie all over. There wasn't hate
in my heart. But my initial reflex was shock and embarrassment. I
didn't know what to do. Bob quickly said, ''Don't touch the guy.
Let him go.'' Then Bob said, almost in the same breath, ''Anita,
let's pray.'' I was encouraged by the honest reporting of the
incident in the media. One media clipping that came to my attention has been a source of encouragement. In it, the reporter questioned, ''When we don't stand up for morality, aren't we, in a
way, telling others that we approve?'' He then went on to explain
that it really wouldn't take too many standing up for their beliefs
to bring the silent masses to their feet, and then we could see our
beliefs put into action. He asked another question. ''Aren't moral
standards worth standing up for?''

The Associated Press reported that comedian Bob Hope had
been asked by Texaco to stop making jokes about me and ''gay''
liberation. Here was a case of the silent masses voicing protest.
And Texaco meant business for which I praise God. Texaco sponsors many of Bob's TV specials. ''Please, please lay off the Anita
Bryant jokes,'' they urged, because ''customers are tearing up
their credit cards and sending them back.'' This is the first instance of a type of boycott by concerned Americans and Christians that had come to my attention. Bob Hope, however, *is* one
of my loyal entertainer friends.

Cathy Smith, a news editor for a journal in Coffeyville, Kansas,
wrote: ''Isn't it sad that whenever Anita Bryant's name is
mentioned, a few sneers are put in her direction followed by
several jokes and 'putdowns'?

''It seems that whenever someone tries to fight in favor of
something evil or immoral, several come to their defense, and
whenever someone stands up for good and moral things, they are

greatly criticized and laughed at.''

Cathy explained that homosexuality was no laughing matter, and if those of us who believe it is wrong don't stand up for what is true and right, it will become more of a problem than this country is prepared to handle. This stands true not only for homosexuality, but for child pornography and other immoral practices.

This news editor pointed out that my job and fame were at stake and my life in danger just because I'd stood up for my beliefs. She pointed out that people like herself, average citizens, don't have that at stake. She found it inconceivable that people who consider themselves to be kindhearted, good, honest people should laugh and toss aside what's happening as though it were nothing.

Plainly, we are up against spiritual warfare in a very worldly arena. It is rare to find a news reporter or editor who understands the implications of what's happening and is willing to go out on a limb and tell it like it is.

The *Wall Street Journal* reported that the Screen Actors Guild has condemned me and our ''homosexual-rights-law campaign spawned in hatred and fueled by fear.'' Actors' Equity Association also took me to task, though other Hollywood notables— Jane Fonda, Marlon Brando, Vanessa Redgrave, to name a few—have been allowed to speak their controversial political pieces in peace. Consider, too, that what I said was not even politically oriented, but was the honest response of a mother's heart to something that affected her children.

It is my own conviction that the reason the Hollywood crowd and entertainers in general have been so hostile is not that they approve so much of homosexuality, but they realize if they condemn homosexual acts, they would have to look at their own lives differently. Because if you stand in opposition to the act of homosexuality, then you have to condemn adultery, promiscuity, fornication and all these acts that God's Word labels sin.

Opponents have been condemning me by urging boycotts,

blacklisting, and other more aggressively violent tactics. One such "gay" paper editorialized: "We should not rest until Anita Bryant is utterly destroyed. Until Anita Bryant has no big house on the bay; until Anita Bryant has no $100,000 a year job; until Anita Bryant is forced to live in an anti-gay ghetto; I have absolutely not one qualm about taking potshots at her. I certainly have no sympathy such as that expressed over the loss of her job, and if there is anything I can do to *cost* her a job, I would have no hesitation to do it. And why not? Is it not but the converse of what Anita Bryant intends for us . . . . It is an unquestioned maxim of herd psychology that on attack you go for the leader, be it a herd of elephants, cattle, or, as in this case, a wolf pack. Anita Bryant is the *only* place to attack Anita Bryant and her followers. That maxim applies at least equally to warfare, for to bring down the leader is to demoralize and confuse those who would follow . . . . And, so long as Anita Bryant continues her genocidal attack on gays, with no reprisal whatsoever . . . we have no choice but to 'not rest until Anita Bryant is utterly destroyed.' We have to go after her to bring down our enemies, and we have to go after her to regain our allies . . . ."

The editor outlines his intentions in terms of what he calls "two powerful weapons: *Controversy* . . . and *Boycott* . . ." and he names friends and allies in the forefront of the entertainment world and the influential media (newspapers, TV, and radio) who are lending their time and efforts to help accomplish my destruction.

We have a determined foe. It calls for a mighty show of strength by the hitherto silent masses. We believe that the silent majority in America will not allow this destruction of either me or this nation to take place. The *National Enquirer* (May 23, 1978) says in bold headlines: BACKLASH AGAINST GAY RIGHTS SWEEPS AMERICA. "A backlash against gay rights legislation is sweeping the nation. It's spearheaded by citizens demanding a return to morality and decency in society, top psychiatrists say." The article quotes Dr. Harold Voth, senior psychiatrist and psychoanalyst at the Menninger Foundation, Dr. Armand Nicholi, Jr., instructor in psychiatry at the Harvard Medical School, Dr. Martin Grotjahn, professor emeritus at the University of Southern California, and Dr. Charles W. Socarides, clinical professor of psychiatry at the State University of New York's Downstate Medical Center.

The general consensus among these top-echelon professional men is that there has been a sliding morality in this country that's gone too far. Doctor Nicholi, for instance, stated: "There is a general feeling that homosexuals have a right to be accepted as people, but not to demand that homosexuality be accepted as normal." Which is precisely what I have been saying all along.

Doctor Nicholi warns that the more the "gays" try to force this issue, the more backlash they will inspire. If the mail we receive at Protect America's Children is a fair indicator—and we have reason to believe it is—then this psychiatrist is right on.

Doctor Grotjahn concurred: "The current backlash is not people saying, 'I'm against homosexuals.' What they're really saying is 'I'm for decency.' The average man and woman really don't care what others do, as long as they do it quietly. But the homosexuals have made too much noise."

Doctor Socarides emphasized that most people want to be fair to homosexuals. It is the militant homosexuals who have been shouting "unfair," and making other false accusations. Socarides points to the efforts by activists who want to "teach school children that homosexuality is 'normal.' They want to encourage homosexuality even among the youth. They even want to censor textbooks which list homosexuality as a disorder," said this knowledgeable doctor.

Doctor Voth echoed what we have been hearing from grassroots people: "We're just plain fed up . . . ."

People have asked, "Anita, why did you allow an interview for *Playboy* magazine?" The answer is, "I didn't!" The interviewer originally contacted us and, after much deliberation and prayer, in addition to some correspondence, we consented to do an interview with him for *Rolling Stone* magazine.

The same thing happened with a free-lance writer researching an article on homosexuality for the *New York Times.* This writer sold her story to *Penthouse.*

We are constantly subjected to this dilemma. If you refuse to do interviews, you are then almost giving away your access to the media. That is what the opposition wants us to do. We have to make choices. Are we going to say no to all interviews and get hurt by not having our side told; or, shall we grant interviews, being as selective and careful as possible, hoping that people reading out there have, by now, learned to realize that what they are seeing is not always accurate reporting of what we have, in fact, said?

The Lynchburg, Virginia, *Daily Advance* asked: "What's a nice girl like Anita Bryant doing in the spicy *Penthouse* magazine?" They answered that by printing the truth as we had explained it to them. We have no control over free-lance writers who tell us one thing, and then turn around and do something else. We have consulted with attorneys when we have discovered that we were misinformed. There has been no legal way publication of such interviews in magazines not of our choosing can be blocked. The *Daily Advance* editorial said: "We're inclined to think Anita might have reached quite a few people she might not have reached otherwise. Surely, her religious commitment and her concept of decency in America are reported in full in *Penthouse.* The article itself does nothing to diminish Miss Bryant.

"Neither she nor Bob is sure any good can come from the writer's report, but they agree there is the possibility through a different audience . . . . Anita might have made some converts."

In the case of the *Playboy* interview, Bob or someone was with me at all times while I was being interviewed. When the writer accompanied us on four days of travel, we did not know he would report it as "Cruising With Anita."

To Christians who misunderstand, I can only point you to the

Bible which should be our common meeting ground in defense of the truth.

Is there any such thing as Christians cheering each other up? Do you love me enough to want to help me? Does it mean anything to you that we are brothers in the Lord, sharing the same Spirit? Are your hearts tender and sympathetic at all? Then make me truly happy by loving each other and agreeing wholeheartedly with each other, working together with one heart and mind and purpose . . . . You are to live clean, innocent lives as children of God in a dark world full of people who are crooked and stubborn. Shine out among them like beacon lights, holding out to them the Word of Life. . . .

Philippians 2:1, 2, 15, 16 LB

The article in *Playboy* came at a bad time for me when I was physically exhausted and had to take off a week and go into hiding, retreating from everyone and everything. This was done under doctor's orders and was one of the most difficult decisions I had to face. It meant cancelling my planned appearance in Saint Paul (Bob went instead and did a fantastic job), and a few other appearances. Entertainers have a saying, "The show must go on," but in this instance, the show didn't go on, and I went away.

While I was gone I had time to think through some of the flak that had come at me from the Christian world in response to the *Playboy* article. The outside world had tried to demolish me; now the Christian world was angry and coming at me—or so it seemed. Before getting away, I felt that I was just barely hanging on by the skin of my teeth. It looked as though God was cutting the cords holding those closest to me and that I was left standing alone. I felt like I'd been abused and used. The doctor said, "If they don't kill you on the outside, you are going to kill yourself on the inside . . . ."

I thought about that and somehow felt he was right, although not necessarily in the way he meant it. But there was a dying of my inner being. The Apostle Paul said that those things he once counted as gain, he now counted as loss for the sake of Christ (*see* Philippians 3:7). The only way to really know Christ and His power, Paul said, was to be ready to suffer and to die for Him if necessary (*see* Philippians 3:10). "I hope all of you who are mature Christians will see eye-to-eye with me on these things, and if you disagree on some point, I believe that God will make it plain to you—if you fully obey the truth you have" (Philippians 3:15, 16 LB).

The Book of Romans also gives much instruction in matters such as this. As I sought God's leading, I grappled with tremendous pressure.

Before getting away for five days, I sat down and wrote a note to Bob urging him to do for us as a family what he felt was best and what needed doing—sell the house, change our life-style, close down Protect America's Children—whatever he decided, I was prepared to accept the decision. "Let me be to you just a wife, and to our children, just a mother . . . ."

Bob took it seriously, but on the other hand, he knew I was reacting from being overtired. "You'd never be happy in retirement, Anita," he said. Still I was unwilling to give up the idea. Then I made the announcement to the kids. Now, in retrospect, I can see that I was trying to deal with my guilt feelings about being away from the children so much. In some ways I was acting like a frightened child.

I thought the children would say, "Hey, Mom, that's great news. You mean you're going to be around home more often!"

Instead, Billy said, "Mother, what about America?"

Barbara looked sad and worried. "Mother, you can't let down all those people who have hope for the first time and who believe in you, and who are looking to you for leadership."

I sat there cringing as I heard these remarks from my children.

Gloria commented, "Now, Mother, you know you're tired and need a good rest. Daddy can let up on your schedule and after some time off, you'll feel differently. And besides, Mom, you're

too young to retire. Do things in moderation, that will settle it.''
I looked over at Bobby who put up his hands and said, ''I don't
want to get in the middle of all this!''

The children's comments helped me get back my balance. They
saw it realistically, and I didn't. It shocked me. I didn't want to
hear it, because I was too tired to go on. I wanted out, and I was
desperately crying for help from my husband and children in the
only way I knew how. And it didn't *appear* that they were taking
me too seriously.

At that moment I took over the management of my own self,
cancelled three important meetings, and went away. Friends flew
in with their own jet and took me to their cabin hideaway. My
friend, who has never had to do any cooking or cleaning on her
own, undertook to cook and care for me by herself. It was a real
labor of love. The cabin overlooked a beautiful lake, and I was
able to settle back and let nature and God do their restorative
work.

I began to realize that the pace we'd been keeping was exacting
a toll. There was a price to pay healthwise as well. It scared me
because I realized that at the rate we'd been going, physically I
was burning myself out. I got the right perspective on the situation finally and even came to understand that I didn't have to feel
guilty about leaving the children. They had always had my time in
quality if not in as much quantity as I'd have liked at all times.
The brief time away from Bob and the children was good for them
as well as for me.

I came to grips with the *Playboy* interview and the reaction of
the public. I had granted the interview in good conscience and
Bob thought he had done a thorough job of screening Ken Kelly,
the writer. His letters had convinced us of his earnestness, and he
even convinced us he was a Christian family man and showed us
pictures of his family. He even wore a wedding ring.

Ed Rowe, our executive director, confronted Kelly on a Miami
radio talk-show program. Ed went prepared with copies of the
letters Kelly had written to us purporting to be a Christian in full

accord with our stand. He had signed over to us editorial rights in three letters, then failed to honor his promise. In the course of their radio confrontation, Ed reported, Kelly became visibly shaken. Face distorted and pitifully unnerved, he whipped out a quart-sized bottle of some kind of alcoholic beverage and started drinking it right in front of the microphone. Rather than face Rowe again, Kelly and his agent cancelled another confrontation on a different station which had been scheduled for the following evening. During the debate with Ed Rowe, he admitted that he had done an extremely heavy editing job on the transcript of the taped interview.

Kelly's "editing" brought our way some of the most severe criticism that we have taken through all of the homosexual-issue storm. On the talk-show program, Ed showed the duplicity of Ken Kelly in trying to make me look anti-Semitic. Kelly had made it appear that I hate Jews and that I had singled out and assigned them to hell.

The Bible teaches that those who reject Jesus Christ are lost and doomed to separation from Him in heaven. There is a heaven, and there is a hell. The idea did not originate with me. God has provided a way of salvation, and if men choose to reject this plan, then they are going to have to pay the penalty—non-Jews, as well as Jews. It has nothing to do with a person's ethnic background.

Kelly's "editing" also distorted my response to his question about imprisonment for homosexual acts. I never said that homosexuals should get twenty years in prison, but Ken Kelly kept baiting me to say it. In interviewing he said it several times. I believe that "hawks," men who round up young boys, "chickens" to use and abuse, should receive felony sentences. As I have stated before, watering down the law is not the answer to reducing crime—any crime—nor is it a deterrent to homosexual practices and other acts of immorality.

In the final analysis, God Himself is the Judge of all motives—mine as well as others—and He does know my heart. While I may be no match for the godless who set out to make me look ridiculous (and often succeed), I have confidence that the Holy Spirit can work through me (as weak a vessel as I am), and I am willing to take the risk if God can be glorified and if perchance someone might come to Christ as a result.

I read Romans 10 where Paul says:

> But how shall they ask him to save them unless they believe in him? And how can they believe in him if they have never heard about him? And how can they hear about him unless someone tells them?
>
> v. 14 LB

I am willing to be that "someone." But many times I have questioned, "Why me, Lord?" I may not do as good a job as a theologian who has all the right answers and verses at his fingertips, but for some reason, God has allowed me to be used. Someone has to speak up on these issues which are threatening our nation's families. "Hast thou faith? have it to thyself before God. Happy is he that condemneth not himself in that thing which he alloweth" (Romans 14:22).

The Apostle could say he was responsible to no mere man and that was his answer to those who questioned his rights and his judgment on certain matters (*see* 1 Corinthians 9). He knew God had picked him out and given him a sacred trust (*see* v. 17). ". . . whatever a person is like, I try to find common ground with him so that he will let me tell him about Christ and let Christ save him. I do this to get the Gospel to them . . ." (vv. 22, 23 LB).

On the first anniversary of the repeal of the Dade County ''gay rights'' ordinance, Anita and Bob announce plans to start a counseling ministry to homosexuals to be set up through Anita Bryant Ministries. (Wide World Photos)

Acting on her conviction that God has given her a message to deliver to all Christians, Anita continues to sing and give her testimony as she did at the Pittsburgh Civic Center. (Bill Levis, Pittsburgh *Post-Gazette*) *Below:* Anita greets those attending the Southern Baptist Pastor Conference where she reminded the 21,000 attendants that those who do not stand for moral issues will have to answer to God. (Wide World Photos)

"A little gal born in Barnsdall," Anita addresses the Oklahoma State Senate, telling legislators that citizens are crying out for moral men and women to be elected to state and national offices. At left is Senate President Pro Tem Gene Howard, and at right, Senator John Luton. (Wide World Photos) *Right:* State Senator Mary Helm, who invited Anita to address the legislators, is the author of a bill which would allow school boards to fire teachers who advocate homosexual activities or engage in "public homosexual activity." (Courtesy of Hal Lewis, state photographer, State of Oklahoma)

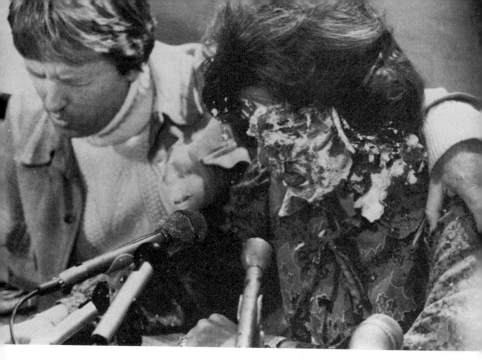

"Don't touch the guy. Let him go," said Bob before leading Anita to pray for the self-professed homosexual who smacked Anita with a pie at a press conference in Des Moines, Iowa. (Wide World Photos) *Below:* While promoting *The Anita Bryant Story,* Anita tells newsman Edwin Newman about the cancelled appearances, both in concerts and on TV, as a result of bomb threats and demonstrations on the part of "homosexual rights" supporters. (Wide World Photos)

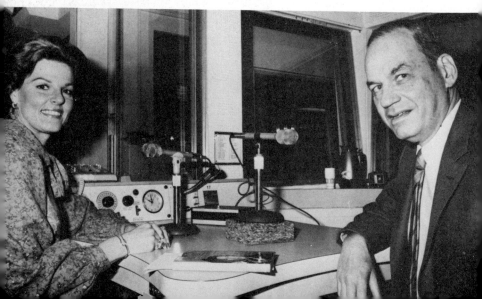

Cecil Todd, director of Revival Fires, Joplin, Missouri, and Anita and Bob discuss the aim of Revive America Crusades to urge citizens to uphold the biblical standards of morality in compassionate and caring ways.

Right: "Wauchula represents the heartbeat of America, and I just wanted to see what you look like in person," Anita told the standing-room-only crowd at the Revive America Crusade in this Florida community. (*Herald-Advocate*, Wauchula, Florida)

The Reverend Ken Campbell welcomed Anita to Toronto where
she helped launch the Christian Liberation Crusade, emphasizing
that her purpose in coming was to spread the Gospel, not to
campaign against homosexuals. (Courtesy Paul Wodehouse, Bur-
lington, Canada) *Below:* Charles Colson and Anita participated in
the sunrise Easter service in Miami Marine Stadium where Colson told worshipers, "Jesus Christ offers us the way to live with
ourselves, the way to live with God, the way to live with our
neighbors, and the way to live with society." (Pelham & William-
son)

In Houston, Anita sang to a member of the American Farm Bureau Federation which gave her a standing ovation. (Wide World Photos) *Below:* However, the night before, "homosexual rights" supporters rallied outside to proclaim their so-called civil rights. (Wide World Photos)

Bob Hope and Anita entertained for the benefit of the Welborn Baptist Hospital Foundation in Evansville, Indiana. They were met backstage by Red Skelton. (*Evansville Press*) *Left:* "If from my experience others can be helped and challenged to stand for what is right, then share we must," reaffirms Anita. For her, the day of the comfortable Christian is over. (Wide World Photos)

8
Contrary Winds

> Jesus Christ is no security *against* storms, but He is
> perfect security *in* storms. He has never promised you
> an easy passage, only a safe landing.
>
> MRS. CHARLES E. COWMAN
> *Streams in the Desert*

When I read "Controversial Anita Bryant . . ." I get uptight. Do
you ever read "Controversial Gays"?

I, along with others, am disturbed that we've allowed the
homosexuals to take over good words like the word *gay* itself.
The so-called "gays" own the word *gay* now, it seems. People
are even reluctant to sing the Christmas song that says, "Don we
now our gay apparel . . . ." Ridiculous!

And there is the word *discriminate*. That's a good word. It used
to be good to be a discriminating person. It means to show per-
ception and good taste. Not so anymore. We should be more
discriminating in our life-style, if it is not for the good of our
families and the welfare of society. Since when is it wrong to say
no to something that is immoral? I'll tell you when it's wrong; it
has become wrong because we've allowed the militant-
homosexual element in society to take over the word and spoil its
meaning.

People are always asking us how we feel about these and other
things. The answer is *strongly!*

Someone accused me of being a "reviler" because I wiped pie

over the homosexual's face in the parking lot "off camera," as
the critic said. The dictionary tells me that a "reviler" is someone
who uses abusive language. This same columnist said I should
start worrying about being a "dropout from the Kingdom [of
heaven]." ". . . Vengeance is mine; I will repay, saith the
Lord" (Romans 12:19). University of Chicago theologian Martin
E. Marty suggests that if we are going to be Bible literalists, then
we should be literally literal. Someone else said they felt the Lord
used my hand to do the repaying in this instance. I can't think of a
single instance—either before that episode or since—when either
Anita or I have shown vengeance. We have not sought to strike
back. *Retribution* is not a word in our vocabulary, nor the word
revile.

I find it disturbing to see those in Miami and elsewhere who are
making a fortune off the homosexual issue. There are "centers"
where for a price you can participate in so-called "learning experiences" where you are taught techniques and principles for
dealing with people in same-sex and both-sex relationships in
order to facilitate complete interpersonal relating based upon
human-to-human communication away from the closet of gender
roles. Fancy words for degenerate sex.

Workshops are conducted where you can "experience simul-
taneous male-plus-female energy in the form of an individual of
each gender 'sculpting,' 'forming,' and 'creating' the unclothed or
dressed body of a third person." Liberal Christians would have
us believe that this is "human liberation," and those of us holding
to the Bible are "morally immature."

Directions for "workshop" sessions state: "As the hands move
up one's body the discrimination between male and female falls
away and the bodymind naturally integrates the two sets of sensa-
tions into one euphoric transperience . . . . In growth beyond
the taboo of loving two people at once, there is an instant
Woodstock of discoveries beyond jealousy and possessiveness in
which one's body becomes an open channel of emotions between

the other two, losing 'self' and discovering the natural high which is always there.''

Liberal Christian writers state, ''long-accepted standards [regarding morals] must be transcended.''

The Bible states:

Be not deceived; God is not mocked: for whatsoever a man soweth, that shall he also reap. For he that soweth to his flesh shall of the flesh reap corruption; but he that soweth to the Spirit shall of the Spirit reap life everlasting.

Galatians 6:7, 8

And if that's Bible thumping and Bible literalism, then I willingly stand accused.

The Old Testament prophets never flinched in crying out their woes to the rebellious, sinful people. I gladly echo their refrain:

Woe to her [him] that is filthy [rebellious] and polluted . . . . the unjust knoweth no shame.

See Zephaniah 3:1, 5

When you ignore the moral absolutes of the Bible, you have no guidelines left. We have been accused of clutching our righteous robes around us, passing by on the far side of the road (away from homosexuals), and choosing instead the ''path of self-righteous noninvolvement.''

But the moment the Miami newspapers carried a story that we were hosting a two-day brainstorming session involving a former homosexual, a psychologist, two couples from the east coast experienced in working with homosexuals, and other concerned Christians, the local militant homosexuals rose up to protest and tried, in fact, to gain admission. They claimed Anita was going to teach mental health and stated this was ''ludicrous at best.'' The claim was never made that Anita was going to do any such thing.

Once again their big lie has been refuted. One wonders what

lengths they will go to next to try to discredit our efforts at helping homosexuals.

At almost every press conference we get this same question: "Don't you feel that you are exploiting the public by writing a book about the homosexual issue?" The fact that Anita and I have been writing books for years, and that this has long been a phase of our lives, a part of the way we earn our living, is never taken into consideration. I would like to ask, "Who is exploiting the issue for monetary gain?"

For years we in the Christian community have allowed the secular world to back us into a corner as they've made us look like opportunists out to make a fast buck. Phil Donahue and others question Billy Graham, Anita, and other religious leaders, "How much money do you make?" But do you ever hear them ask entertainment figures how much *they* make? If we were to turn around and say, "Tell us how much *you* make, Phil," he might answer, "I make eight zillion dollars; go jump in the lake, Bob Green, it's none of your ——— business what I make!"

We have not been responding correctly. The liberal media and the secular world has a misconception of religion which we have been guilty of fostering because of a weakness in our attitude of response. We have nothing to hide. We feel this moral obligation to be polite and to cooperate, but we need to rethink our strategy. I call upon Christians who are put on the spot like that in the future to confront the media head-on, tell them it's none of their business, or go to the other extreme—exaggerate and call their bluff.

As Christians we are accustomed to "turning the other cheek," (*see* Matthew 5:39). There is a way to do that, however, without a verbal response and that is to refuse to dignify and simply ignore those who ask obviously loaded and silly questions.

A decision has been reached which will have a direct bearing on future press conferences. As Chairman of the Board and Director of Media for Protect America's Children and Anita Bryant Ministries, I shall be lifting some of the burden from Anita's shoulders.

This does not mean Anita will be shielded from participation in interviews and such press conferences, but it does mean she is more free to refrain from responding when put on the spot. Other changes will be noted as the future course of this new and expanding ministry finds its focus.

God has been doing a new work in my heart this past year. I have found direction and help wherever I turn in the Bible, and God's people have poured out their love and concern and have shared ideas that have come to them which might be of benefit to us and the work.

In the course of writing this book I was able to tell Anita that I have learned and am accepting the fact that God uses the abrasive experiences of life to conform us to the image of His Son. Second Corinthians 4 speaks to my heart:

> Therefore seeing we have this ministry, as we have received mercy, we faint not.
>
> V. 1

The Living Bible makes it very plain:

> It is God himself, in his mercy, who has given us this wonderful work [of telling his Good News to others], and so we never give up. We do not try to trick people into believing—we are not interested in fooling anyone. We never try to get anyone to believe that the Bible teaches what it doesn't. All such shameful methods we forego. We stand in the presence of God as we speak and so we tell the truth, as all who know us will agree . . . .
>
> We boldly say what we believe [trusting God to care for us], just as the Psalm writer did when he said, "I believe and therefore I speak."
>
> 2 Corinthians 4:1, 2, 13

Anita is constantly depicted as being "antigay." I would like to suggest to the media that they try labeling her "profamily," "pro-God," "promotherhood," "prolife," "pro-Bible," "pro-morality" and pro- other good things.

Accuracy in the media is a rarity in these days of advocating with adjectives. In the future I shall be more alert to bias and distortion, and I call for fellow Christians to do the same. When you discover it, call or write your newspaper and voice your displeasure. Send us a copy of your letter.

Reed Irvine, reporting in the Fairfax, Virginia, *Falls Church Globe,* called this to the attention of readers. He mentioned "ultraconservatives" such as Senator Jesse Helms who has been a staunch supporter of Anita. Irvine asked, "When was the last time you encountered an 'ultraliberal'?"

Good question! "Apparently there is no such species," he added. "Nor are there any 'extremists' to the left of center—only 'militants' or 'activists.' " We would be labeled extremists—someone passionately holding the wrong views. A militant, on the other hand, is someone who is immoderately pursuing the "correct" ends (according to the media).

The neatest ploy of all is the selective use of the word *controversial.* Anita Bryant therefore is "controversial." Leaders of "gay rights" groups are not.

Irvine warns that the advocacy journalism that is embodied in the adjectives that the writers and broadcasters use is extremely influential. The essence of effective propaganda is constant repetition. Irvine says the time has come to protest this adjectival asymmetry, not only in the broadcasting but in the print media as well.

An avalanche of protest mail to the sponsors of network programs, and to your local newspapers, and to national magazines would get across the message that no longer does (so-called) straight America intend to stand by idly and allow this to continue unchallenged.

Irvine calls attention to reports on conflicts that appear from time to time between feminist and "antifeminist" women. Anita would be labeled an "antifeminist" practicing "scare" tactics, making "farfetched" charges, "misrepresenting" the ERA, and "lobbying" legislators. The feminists, of course, do none of those nasty things. "They are merely going to 'analyze the political situation in each state and organize.' "

This astute writer has called something to our attention that it would be well for us to heed. "Keep an eye out for code words such as these," he cautions. "They are worth complaining about." This is something we can all participate in and know that we are making a positive and tangible contribution to help right the wrongs that have taken place in this nation for too long by those who are opinion molders.

There is also a movement underway to eliminate "sexist" language from the Bible. You can guess who is spearheading that!

As Christians, we need to learn to use the Bible today in today's world—not only in prayer and religious matters, but in everyday life. What an enormous burden would be lifted from us. Anita and I have experienced this; we have learned how up-to-date the Bible is through all that we have experienced. We see it as contemporary and relevant. We have not been left powerless; we can use it as a defensive weapon that turns into an offensive weapon. When Jesus didn't answer questions, it was the smartest offensive weapon He could have chosen. When we, as Christians, are confronted with questions that are meant to be embarrassing, and when untruths and lies are thrown at us, and when Scripture is quoted out of context to us, rather than to deny categorically things that are said, we would all be better off not to answer the accuser who, in reality, is none other than the devil himself.

When the storms come, I think of Jesus and His disciples on the storm-tossed sea. The Bible says ". . . the wind was contrary" (Matthew 14:24). Peter dared to walk on that troubled sea. Do I?

In *The Open Bible* footnotes I found something that has been a steadying force when I am confronted with the waves that threaten to overwhelm. Peter did the impossible thing; he walked on the water, by faith. Next, Peter did the conceivable thing: he saw the storm, and had a second thought—he doubted.

For a moment, he lost sight of Jesus.

Then Peter did the natural thing: he feared destruction. Doubt always breeds fear.

Peter did the expected thing: he began to sink—he failed.

Now Peter did the right thing: he prayed, "Lord, save me." Immediately Jesus stretched forth His hand and caught him. Once more Peter made contact with Jesus by faith.

"All of us need a faith that is bigger than the elements we confront that would drag us down to defeat" (The Open Bible).

Bob Green needs to pray daily: Lord, give me the faith of a Peter who dared to step out and walk on the water to go to You. And, Lord, continue to teach me and show me how to handle the contrary winds.

9
What's Going On in America?

> . . . I am set for the defence of the gospel.
> Philippians 1:17

WHAT'S GOING ON IN AMERICA? That was the headline on a two-page ad which appeared in *Time* magazine, spelling out Dutch reaction to what one newspaper described as "Florida's anti-homosexual campaigner Anita Bryant." The ad cost forty thousand dollars and was paid for by a sell-out celebrity concert, entitled "The Miami Nightmare." It was held in Amsterdam's Concertgebouw.

We must have stepped on some international toes to have provoked that kind of response from across the ocean!

There were scores of leading Dutch entertainers who volunteered their services for the all-night event to raise the necessary funds for that ad. Joining the entertainers were leaders of most of Holland's major political parties—some of whom have publicly proclaimed their own homosexuality. Everyone who spoke called what is happening in America a denial of "basic human rights."

What's going on in America? *Time* magazine (May 22, 1978) reported "a backlash against growing tolerance," in its summation of voting in Wichita and Saint Paul to overturn the "gay rights" ordinances in those communities. The magazine reported the "vote caused tremors among gays from San Francisco to New York."

Civil libertarians, of course, saw the repeal vote as "an unwelcome suppression of minority rights. Said Presidential Assistant Margaret Costanza: 'The voters go in the booth and think they're saying they don't approve of homosexuality. But they're not. They're saying that anyone's human rights can be taken away with the pull of a lever.' " *Time* took exception to Costanza and the libertarians and reported, "It seemed more likely that Wichita voters were less interested in restricting the rights of gays than in blocking a community-wide endorsement of a practice they abhor." They also reported the comment of theologian Martin E. Marty: "The American people have had and will continue to have a growing tolerance for homosexual expression. But there is a big difference between a growth in tolerance and a willingness to legislate homosexuality as a normal alternative." Marty is *not* known among "right" evangelicals as being in full accord with their more literal interpretation of the Bible. His comment is, in all probability, quite reflective of the general feeling in the nation among those who adhere to what is being called a "center" and "left" evangelical way of thinking.

There has been a very definite turn in the manner in which some magazines and newspapers are now reporting events surrounding the issue of homosexuality. At the tenth Annual Charismatic Conference of Greater Pittsburgh where I spoke in early June 1978, a reporter began her assessment of me by stating, "She is not anti any group. She is anti-sin . . . sin of all types."

I was criticized in some Christian circles for appearing in Pittsburgh, but I felt God had given me a message that He wanted me to take to all Christians, my brothers and sisters in Christ regardless of the "label" they might wear—fundamentalist, charismatic, Catholic, or whatever. I talked about the need for each of us to be willing in love to bridge the gap and related how, from the very beginning, we have felt that God was using us to knit together the many religious groups and individuals. I am not identified with the charismatic movement, but that was a glorious evening.

College campuses have entered the fray in the continuing debate about homosexuality. A student at Indiana University took it upon himself to write a rebuttal to an article which appeared in the campus paper. The original article was called "an opinionated essay" in which the writer accused me of making a farce of Christian love and those who support our efforts as making a travesty of freedom.

The student's rebuttal stated: "While it is true that the belief in Christ is based on respect and love, when reading further we find that part of that respect and love includes admonishing. The apostle Paul and others repeatedly stress to the early church the importance of admonishing as a *true* display of Christian love (i.e., Colossians 1:28; Romans 15:14; 2 Timothy 4:2). Also important is the fact that admonishing was done both to keep people from sin and to notify or reprove those in fault. Furthermore, Christ Himself provides the model for admonishing as He reproves those who sinned and yet He died that they might be saved."

The student expressed surprise that someone could criticize me with a misrepresentation of the same Scripture that gives me the authority to do so. "If you accept the scripture about a loving God, you must also accept the words of the same scripture that says obedience to His Word is the proper response to the salvation that He offers through faith (it doesn't come by 'being a good person').

"If scripture is used to determine whether Anita Bryant is correct in admonishing people with regard to homosexuality, at least get the scripture right . . . . Though salvation is offered regardless of any sin (as Anita Bryant continually stresses), obedience is not characterized by continued sin."

We appreciate those who take the time and make the effort to refute media distortions.

A pastor wrote his local newspaper calling for more responsible journalism and called a letter which had appeared in a previous issue of the same paper "pure hogwash." It seems a homosexual pastor had written to report that twenty-two churches had been firebombed and thirty-two people had died since I came on the scene to "harass homosexuals." The pastor did some investigative reporting on his own, calling the FBI, the New Orleans Sheriff's Department, and the New Orleans Police Information Bureau, and found the homosexual pastor's claim totally false.

When we were in Pennsylvania, we were met by thirty demonstrators. One of the fellows was dressed as a skeleton carrying a sign with a statement that had previously been attributed to me (widely printed and reported). Bob asked him how he knew I had made that statement. "Because I read it in *Newsweek* magazine," was his reply (as if *Newsweek* were the infallible Bible).

Another problem which we have encountered that has generated much hate and distrust toward us, has come as a result of statements made by politicians, some Christian leaders, and some Christians in general—statements attributed to me which were never made by me. Reporters, in their attempts to reach me for comments, will seek out others for statements—some who for one reason or another may have been connected, even remotely, with me or Protect America's Children. Many times these individuals, who are unaccustomed to handling the media, get "backed into a corner," as it were, and statements are wrested from them when they are put on the spot. Still, it becomes a reflection on me. It becomes a very difficult problem. Even my (straight) hairdresser has been approached for comments. Friends whose names are mentioned in some of our books receive calls and are asked questions. The crank calls to us, to our office, to the church, and to our friends have been innumerable.

A gentleman called the office one day saying it was imperative that he speak with Mr. Bob Green immediately—that it was of utmost importance. The girls try to screen all calls, but this man was so persistent and would not talk to anyone but Bob. He finally told us he was an investigator with the government and gave us a number to return the call. When we called back we found out it was the health department. Bob got on the phone, and the gentleman said Bob's name had been given to them by a man who was reported to have VD. The man claimed he'd been having a homosexual relationship with my husband! The health department explained that they have to call and warn people to get to their doctor for treatment when they receive such reports. Bob then explained that he was my husband. This was just another example of lies meant to discredit us.

Wherever we go we are confronted with the usual placard-carrying demonstrators. We have been keeping an unofficial sort of list of some of the different banners and placards. You have seen them in the press coverage, of course, but here are some you may have missed: RELIGIOUS BIGOTRY KILLS; SAVE CHIL-DREN FROM HUNGER, RACISM, WAR, UNEMPLOYMENT, PREJ-UDICE, SEXISM, AND ANITA; CHILDREN HAVE THE RIGHT TO BE FREE *not* TO BE SAVED; THE GODDESS LOVES US; LET SHE WHO HAS NOT SINNED CAST THE FIRST ORANGE; TODAY HOMOSEXUALS— TOMORROW THE WORLD (at the bottom right of it was a swastika); JUDGE NOT WHAT YOU DON'T UNDERSTAND; IF ANITA'S MOTHER HAD BEEN PRO-ABORTION, WE WOULDN'T HAVE TO BE HERE TO-DAY; RELIGIOUS BIGOTRY IS UNORIGINAL SIN; LOVE IS ABORTION RIGHTS; DON'T PREY ON ME; IT'S A NATURAL WE DIDN'T NEED TO BE TAUGHT; FREEDOM WITHIN OUR HEADS AND ON OUR BEDS; and there are hundreds of others.

We have many letters testifying to the change that has taken place when the Holy Spirit was given access to the homosexual's heart. Letters similar to this one: "I praise God that He has blessed the world with you, even if the unrighteous refuse to see and hear. I am a former homosexual. I was led to the Lord in February 1977. I just want to encourage you to fight onward, and I want you to know that I and hundreds of other former homosex-uals stand with you. You have been an encouraging force in my personal struggle. I thank you. Keep on the armor and keep up the fight." (His reference to armor comes from Ephesians 6:10–20.)

Another letter that is representative of those we receive, is from a former Lesbian. Although it is long, I reprint it here because it tells a dramatic story:

Dearest Sister Anita,

I just finished watching the PTL program and hearing your witness. I felt that I must write and share with you what your courage, in Christ, has done in my life.

I am a born-again Christian, but I had been living in a homosexual relationship since 1973. At that time, I was active in a community church.

I was all wrapped up in "gay rights," but no matter how much rationalization, "logic," reasoning, how many excuses I could come up with, I could not reconcile my life-style with Scripture. I could never get rid of that nagging doubt that kept saying "Hey, you *know* this isn't right."

For four years I lived with one woman, feeling guilty, and trying to justify that relationship to myself. I fully believed that my "gay" nature could not be changed, and that I would always be "gay."

When all the uproar began over the Dade County ordinance, I read everything I could get my hands on about it, and about you. On the one hand, you were a threat to me and my friends; but on the other hand, I respected you tremendously for having the courage of your convictions to stand up in the face of great public ridicule and say what you believed in. It would have been so easy for you to back down.

I saw all those articles quoting you as saying homosexuals *don't have to stay* homosexual, they *can* change, there *is* hope, God still *loves* you. And I read them, and read them again, and again. And I thought, really? Do you really think so? And God, with all His love, brought me to the point in my life where I knew I couldn't continue riding the fence—I had to choose.

I left that relationship, sharing with her why I felt I had to, quit my job, and made preparations to leave the state, to leave all wrong relationships, unchristian friendships and associates behind. I have turned it all over to the Lord, and am trusting Him to cleanse me of all wrong desire, and to create in me a new desire for what is good and right in His sight.

I want to be able to tell people what Jesus has done in my life, and to share with people how great God's love is, and do anything I can to the glory of God. I just want to thank you for being a faithful servant, and planting the seed of hope in my life that was so important. You never know whose life you will touch just by being obedient to Him . . . .

I communicated with this dear woman and thanked her for her precious letter and the encouragement *she* brought into *my* life. I was grateful to be able to tell her that one letter like hers brings enough joy and gladness to offset a thousand more hostile ones.

In answer to the *Time*-magazine ad and the inquiry from the supposedly concerned Dutch people, I would like to relate that these are some of the things that are going on in America. I wish it were possible for our critics as well as supporters and grass-roots Americans to spend a day or two with Bob and me and our children. I would like you to see the relieved reaction of the children when we return home safely and for you to read their little love notes awaiting our arrival.

Gloria, our daughter, admits she's not the world's greatest poet, but I treasure the verse she wrote simply entitled "I Love You."

When you are not home at all, I very well can say,
That I am not too happy, through the livelong day.
I wait 'til you come home, 'til after dark or so,

And when I know you're near, I just about can cheer.
But after you are here, my mind turns round and round,
That I should be bad, and my heart touches the ground.
But then, after you leave, my heart comes in place,
For then I'm very sad, for the time when I was bad.
For I'll never know if I should see my loving parents again,
For I don't even know if they are returning and when.

Welcome Home!
Love,
Gloria and company

A big lump came in my throat when I came across a little letter Gloria's pen pal had written to her in which he'd stated, in response to something she had written, the following: "Yes, the day may come when we will have to stand up for our beliefs too. I hope I can be as brave as your mother."

What's going on in America? Let me tell you what we have discovered is happening in Las Vegas. There it is reported that a certain entertainment couple have made it big on the nightclub circuit with "clever satires and parodic wit" and "stinging cuts at mores and 'myths,' " particularly their mocking anthem to me entitled "We Don't Want Your Children."

But let me tell you, God willing, the flaunting homosexuals in this country who go around crying "human rights, civil rights" aren't going to have my children or the children of other Americans so long as God gives me breath, stamina, and His strength to carry on. The worst thing I could have done for my children, and for other parents' children, is *not* to have stood up for what I believe.

I can't forget the big red-headed kid Freddy Helms who came up to me in Chicago where we kept a booking we'd had with the International Paper Company for three years in a row. It was in honor of the 4-H Clubs of America. We appreciated the fact that they didn't cancel. We kept a low profile and didn't allow a press conference. And it wasn't advertised that we'd be there, nonetheless the homosexuals were out picketing, about seventy-five of them. We looked down from our hotel room, and there were the usual demonstrators with the media. I turned to Bob and said, "This isn't fair. These kids have worked hard for the honors they are going to receive tonight, and now all this is going to detract from them."

It was after the show that the big six-foot-four-inch fellow came up and said, "I hope I did the right thing, Miss Bryant."

I looked up at him and asked, "What do you mean?"

He replied, "Well, when I saw the demonstrators out there, it really upset me. I just marched out across the street and started talking to them and to the newsmen. I told them I didn't think it was fair what they were doing—just showing off and drawing attention to something that was immoral and a sin. I told them we kids had worked hard all year for the honors that were going to be awarded, and that you had a right to stand up for your convictions, just as much as they had a right to theirs, but at least you didn't go around picketing. Besides, that wasn't what you were here for—you weren't here to talk about homosexuality. I asked the newsmen why they didn't film the awards instead—that was something decent and well-earned. If they wanted to focus on something newsworthy, how about zeroing in on something decent for a change . . . ."

When he said that, I asked, "You what?"

"I couldn't help it, Miss Bryant," he started apologizing. "I prayed, and I knew I just had to do it. I hope I did the right thing. I've only been a Christian six months, but I really love God, and I believe what the Bible says. I just had to go out and tell those guys the truth."

I reached up, hugged his neck, and said, "God bless you, boy. You are an answer to prayer, and you have made my day."

His friends came around wanting autographs and some said, "May I shake your hand, Miss Bryant? I sure admire you for standing up for what is right." It was tremendous, and I'll tell you my eyes were full of tears. These kids are the real representatives of America's youth. What's going on in America? There are events like this going on where decent, law-abiding, morally upright young people are showing that some of the people in this nation of ours still know right from wrong.

After doing another *Phil Donahue Show* in Chicago, a pastor picked us up and drove us to South Bend, Indiana, for a concert. On the way he told us a couple of housewives wanted to do something positive, and he told us to watch the left-hand side of the road after we went through a certain underpass just before entering South Bend. There they were—two young gals with babies in each arm! One was standing on top of the car and the other on the bumper, and they had a big sign which read: WELCOME ANITA, WE LOVE YOU! It was a moving experience for me. That night at the concert I told about the two young mothers, and said I recognized that this was a tangible way they had of showing their support and saying, "Thanks Anita, for standing up for America's children." This was during cold weather, too, and the memory of those mothers doing that has buoyed me up many times since then.

Tom Brokaw on *Today* asked me whether I thought homosexuality should be returned to felony status. To these and others who have questioned me on this, I have repeatedly stated that I believe in God's laws as outlined in the Bible, and that the law of the land should be in alignment with the Word of God. Brokaw interrupted me several times as I tried to establish that I am not an expert on law, and that there are no easy answers to tough questions like this.

The Associated Press story which came out following that program was headlined ANITA ASKS U.S. GAY BAN. Such a distortion of what I, in fact, said is commonplace.

Rabbi Phineas Weberman, who endeared himself to me when we stood together in Dade County to defeat the "gay rights" referendum, came to my defense when *Playboy* magazine and others in the media lashed out at me because of certain statements I made (which were actually quoted out of context). He said, "It seems to me interviewers could perhaps have gotten hold of a theological scholar to discuss these things, rather than Anita, who doesn't claim to be such a scholar . . . ."

Rabbi Weberman's statement applies to the many varying questions of a more theological nature which are often thrown at me by the press. Mine is a simple faith, and I can only express it in simple terms. Rabbi Weberman expressed our feelings when he stated: "There should be common ground, a common stand on moral issues, while at the same time allowing a diversity on the theological dogma and learning to respect each other's opinion in that area."

Richard F. Lovelace, a theologian for whom I have much respect, points out in his book *Homosexuality and the Church* the long-held traditional stance of the church, quoting such early church fathers as Augustine who wrote in *Confessions:* "Those shameful acts against nature, such as were committed in Sodom, ought everywhere and always to be detested and punished. If all nations were to do such things, they would equally be guilty of the same crime by the law of God, which has not so made men that they should use one another in this way."

Lovelace cites Martin Luther who considered the prevalence and toleration of homosexual activity among the clergy of his day as one of the worst symptoms of decay in the church, a product of human failure to know and honor the true God. Luther, in his *Commentary on Genesis,* interpreted the prevalence of both heterosexual and homosexual immoralities as forms of vice, giving evidence of the spiritual dereliction of the unreformed church. To which I would add that it is also plainly a moral and spiritual problem for those who make no attachment to any church. Thus the solution for all is to be found in the spiritual realm.

History has left us some lessons. The question is, will we learn from them? What we are faced with in the country, it seems to me, is the undeniable fact that for the pseudo-rights of some, we *all* stand to lose what are truly human rights.

Thank you, America, for standing tall for *your* rights.

10
Are We Headed for Enlightenment or Deterioration?

> Homosexual practices are always an injury done to the Creator, whether or not any offence is at the same time committed against one's neighbor, since they violate His creative intent for human behavior and destroy the beauty of His work.
>
> THOMAS AQUINAS

"Are we watching the further enlightenment of the church or are we seeing the deterioration of Biblical authority?" asks Don Williams in his searching book *The Bond That Breaks: Will Homosexuality Split the Church?*

If anyone has been confronted with the issue as it really is throughout our nation as well as in Canada, it would be quite generally agreed, I presume, that it's been Anita and me. While this book was in the process of being written, Anita issued a statement to the press because of misunderstandings which arose because of magazine interviews. Anita said, "I want to reaffirm my strong conviction that the survival of our nation depends upon the preservation of our Judeo-Christian heritage." Anita and I have consistently tried to enlighten the citizens of this country to the facts and motivation behind the so-called "gay rights" movement. Rather than undermine and dilute those efforts, theologians and believers should unite to sound the warning that moral decay, if allowed to go on unchecked, will signal the deterioration and destruction of what was conceived to be a godly nation.

As social scientists attempt to discuss the true nature of homosexuality, we have seen theologians in particular swept into the maze of thinking. That the influence of the social scientists and theologians is great cannot be denied. But the result, sadly, has been a division among the ranks of believers. Rather than enlightening the church which looks to them for guidance, many theologians have contributed to the confusion and the deterioration of biblical authority.

That some believers need to adopt a more compassionate stance and need enlightenment is not denied. But we deplore that which turns the believer from the whole counsel of God. It is necessary to be compassionate, to be tolerant and sensitive to people's rights—which Anita has been all along—but not at the expense of abandoning one's Christian convictions. To do so is to fall into the hands of those who are out to win converts to their immoral way of life.

A chaplain at a hospital in Illinois pinpointed accurately the substance of the issue, that is, the insistence by proponents for "gay rights" that the homosexual life-style is a natural and normal one. It is an indisputable fact that the homosexual life-style is incapable of reproduction and doomed to certain extinction. In a real sense, it is not a life-style but a "death-style." This chaplain says, "There is certainly no one so optimistic, regardless of life-style, as to imagine God will bless a so-called marriage between homosexuals with new life. God has very cleverly engineered the begetting of life through heterosexual sex and its nourishment through food. To insure the continuity of life, God combines the incentive of pleasure and purpose both in the case of sex and food. When a society or a segment of society becomes so obsessed in its passionate desire for pleasure to the exclusion of purpose, it is taking things out of context which is annoying to its author. In this case the Author is God. For its own survival the homosexual community must of necessity be a parasite drawing life from the heterosexual society which is truly the only natural and normal one.''

Anita poses a threat to the life-style of homosexuals because of her persistent urging that we need to protect America's children from the unnatural aspirations of the radical homosexuals. Unsuspecting and unknowing citizens have been lulled into thinking that it's all right for homosexuals to do whatever they want to each other, that they aren't out to get children, and that they are therefore entitled to inclusion in human-rights codes in cities throughout the country which will assure their receiving preferential treatment. At the same time we, as parents, are being asked to write off our rights.

I can show the reader files of documented accounts of men ''loving'' boys and pornographic material produced by a nationwide lucrative industry—this is big business. Full-grown men taking advantage of children is what we're talking about. It is clearly an obscene use of power where untold physical and psychic violence is inflicted upon children.

By adopting a lenient attitude toward flaunting homosexuals and giving in to their demands, we are paving the way for an influx of social ills the likes of which the average American cannot even imagine. Part of the problem stems from the fact that those advocating leniency and unqualified love toward homosexuals don't know what is going on because they don't make a habit of browsing in adult book shops. They haven't seen the kind of materials that our Protect America's Children office receives, nor have they been subject to the kinds of abuse which Anita has taken.

In answer to author Don Williams's question concerning the further enlightenment of the church or the deterioration of biblical authority, an administrator of a school in California, where homosexuality has made inroads into the school systems and where the present governor openly advocates special rights and privileges for homosexuals, says: "The Bible today has lost nearly all authority within American society, or else it has been twisted by the very libertines it condemns into meaningless doubletalk." This school administrator voices the feelings of other deeply concerned school principals and teachers when he calls homosexuality a "moral cancer."

The late Dr. L. Nelson Bell (father of Mrs. Billy Graham) wrote on the subject of what must be the church's role if it·is to help turn the tide of moral deterioration in this nation. He said:

> We as a nation have become so inured to sin, so complacent in the face of obsession with sex and of the horrible disease of sex deviation, that the judgment of God on us as a people may be very near. This judgment may be swift or it may come slowly with the inexorable certainty of night-fall.
>
> Those who have seen depictions of homosexual orgies in the ruins of Pompeii need very little imagination to understand why that "culture" was doomed to destruction. The Apostle Paul speaks clearly of man's downward course in the first chapter of Romans. From verse 18 to the end of the chapter the progression of human sin is spelled out. Men have denied God's revelation of Himself, says Paul. Consequently they have become fools even while claiming wisdom. In their foolishness they have worshiped the creature rather than the Creator, and God has given them up to their own devices. At the end of the list, as a sort of climax to the whole, the Apostle mentions sexual deviation.
>
> But, as no man is beyond God's love and proferred redemption, so there is yet time for America to repent and turn back to Him. At such a time as this our pulpits should shift from social engineering to soul engineering—proclaiming the lost condition of men out of Christ, the fact that the wages of

sin is death, that the God of love is also the God of holiness and justice and that for those who reject His Son a dreadful day will come. Those apart from God will one day learn that "our God is a consuming fire," and that "it is a fearful thing to fall into the hands of the living God."

Unless the Gospel is preached faithfully those to whom it has been committed will have much to answer for. Unless the Church renews her emphasis on the God of judgment as well as of redemption she will not be true to the Gospel.

The moral apathy of our nation denotes a spiritual sickness which may be fatal. Ancient wisdom speaks to us today: "He who says to the wicked 'You are innocent,' will be cursed by peoples, abhorred by nations; but those who rebuke the wicked will have delight, and a good blessing will be upon them" (Proberbs 24:24, 25 RSV).

Doctor Joseph C. Rupp, a medical examiner in Corpus Christi, Texas, can supply the answer to the question of whether we are headed for enlightenment or deterioration. He states in the journal *Medicine, Science and the Law*: "Within the past decade there has been a rapid deterioration of ethical and moral standards in the United States and radical changes in our attitudes towards sexual matters. During this time the homosexuals in America have taken advantage of the declining morality and general social upheaval and have become another militant minority group." As a medical examiner called upon to investigate sudden unexpected and violent deaths, this doctor has come to realize that the "male homosexual is prone to this type of death with much greater frequency than the average citizen." The information he supplied does not make for pleasant reading.

This medical examiner said, "There is a tired joke in the 'gay' world which goes something like this: 'Show me a happy homosexual, and I'll show you a 'gay' corpse!' " The doctor makes the observation: "As is the case with most sick jokes it makes mirth of a frightening truth." The clandestine nature of the "gay" world, and the perverse activities, finally become more degradation than the homosexual can stand, and suicide is frequently the result. "Youth and good looks are the *sine qua non* of the homosexual and their loss is a major tragedy. To be thirty in the 'gay' world is to already be old. Not infrequently an 'old auntie,' as they are referred to in the 'gay' world, will take his own life . . . ."

This doctor warns about the changing laws which will no longer make homosexual acts, committed by consenting adults in private, a crime. And he states that "the evil of homosexuality is not to be found in the confirmed homosexual adult, but in the subversion and perversion of youth. The homosexual is promiscuous and his attachments fleeting. He is always cruising, looking for fresh young partners. In the gay world, as nowhere else, are youth and good looks at such a premium . . . ." He labels homosexuality a "pernicious and insidious evil."

"Hit a man in his pocketbook and watch him reel into action" is a rephrasing of an old maxim which is applicable today as we confront all the implications of the militant homosexual's quest. The front cover of *New York* magazine, August 1977, showed a scene of me (supposedly) smashing an orange into the face of a model who resembled Anita. The special section was entitled "Gay Clout." Clarke Taylor, journalist, reported that the publisher of *Blueboy* magazine (one of the new slick "gay" magazines) believes the most potentially profitable untapped market in this country is the male homosexual. Taylor asserts, "There are gays in positions of power on Wall Street, Madison, and Seventh Avenues [New York]—this is the invisible gay-power bloc . . . ."

The "gay" market is affluent. "Few gays are bogged down in family support and most are self-sufficient. They will not hesitate to spend money on items they want," *New York* magazine reports. "The potential voting power [of "gays"] is staggering."

Anita and I would be among those lauding the creative talents of homosexuals. We have worked with them in the entertainment industry all our lives. We have had no quarrel with them and what they do in the privacy of their own bedrooms until the Dade County incident.

Letha Scanzoni and Virginia Mollenkott (*Is the Homosexual My Neighbor?*) point to the contributions to civilization by homosexuals and state that society would be impoverished by the loss of the contributions of such people as Michelangelo, Leonardo da Vinci, Christopher Marlowe, James I of England (who commissioned the translation of the Bible that bears his name), Sir Francis Bacon, Walt Whitman, and others. The value of their contributions to society is not being questioned, neither is the potential creativity of today's homosexuals being demeaned, but this does not make their practice of homosexuality right. If these creative people practiced their homosexuality, then according to the biblical standard, they were moral failures.

Bennett J. Sims, an Episcopal bishop, writing in *Christianity Today,* (February 24, 1978, "Sex and Homosexuality") makes an observation that applies here: "The use of one failure to cast more favorable light upon another failure is the first circle in a spiral of collapsing morality." Sims pleads for a church that will stand tall for what we have received and believe, "that the world may know on whom to count for what endures to sustain and nourish human souls."

Such a church is The People's Church in Toronto, Canada, pastored by the world-respected Reverend Paul Smith. (This church is known for its far-flung missionary endeavors.) We went there in January 1978. Anita was very tired; I had overbooked her, and we'd been on the constant go for months. But the experiences in Canada were some of the greatest either of us have ever known. Anita told the gathering, "Quite honestly, I was hesitant to come here . . . . But to see your love and commitment has made it worthwhile." She was introduced (among other things) as being the TV celebrity associated with the Florida orange-juice commercials. To that she responded, "I've come to talk about a vitamin C even better for you than Florida orange juice—and that's Christ. Take Him, and you'll never thirst again.''

In that audience was a woman concealing a cream pie. Despite tight police security, she managed to get in. Shortly after the service ended, she hit the minister, Paul Smith, in the face with the pie. Outside the church that day police estimated five hundred pickets from Toronto's homosexual community turned out to demonstrate. While they recited, "Two, four, six, eight, gay is twice as good as straight," Anita quietly gave her testimony, sang, and shared her concern for a society whose motto is, "If it feels good, do it." Anita stated, "We need to get back to Bible morality."

It was Reverend Ken Campbell, president of Renaissance International, who was instrumental in making arrangements for us to go to Toronto. The *Sunday Sun* (January 15, 1978), one of Toronto's leading papers, reported "There is a totalitarian streak to the anti-Anita campaign—such as Ottawa homosexuals urging Immigration Minister Cullen to deny her entry into Canada . . . . Anita's cardinal sin is that she dares dissent with dissenters. Think about it. While she may have an evangelical fervor that puzzles and makes some feel uneasy, what she really stands for are traditional, Judeo-Christian values . . . . Anita Bryant in Toronto threatens no one's civil liberties. And hers shouldn't be threatened either. Nor should the rights of those who want to hear her speak, sing, whatever. Anita Bryant may even be more welcome than some of those who oppose her."

One woman wrote a letter to the editor of a Toronto paper in which she stated: "I'm a free-thinking agnostic, but I agree that Miss Bryant's fight against the arrogant type of homosexual is well justified. In the face of her militant adversaries and lack of full support from antihomosexuals who fear to speak out because 'prejudice' is a dirty word, her courage is commendable . . . . I object to the kind of homosexuals who try to convince the world, including young children, that their way of life is normal."

Again in the spring of 1978 we traveled to Canada where Anita appeared in concert. Reverend Ken Campbell, who arranged all the meetings, told the press that the issue in Canada is "the battle for the soul of a society."

The demonstrators in Canada were particularly noisy as they screamed their chants and marched in cadence. With placards bobbing up and down, the chants were deafening: "Not the church, not the state, people should decide their fate." One homosexual speaker shouted: "The big threat to us, even more than Anita Bryant, is the growing number of born-again Christians!" A much-repeated phrase of these demonstrators was: "Gay solidarity is our business."

A Lesbian grabbed a mike from the speaker's platform and shouted, "I'm a woman, a socialist, and a Lesbian. Anita Bryant heads a right-wing coalition. She provides a cover for the political people who are the real problem. Too many of them are taken in by Anita Bryant's arguments."

Born-again Christians and right-wing politicians—who is to blame?

A screaming homosexual shouted, "Let's pray for Anita, because she preys on us. We are the Jews and the Muslims and the others that Anita Bryant consigns to hell."

Many of the speakers wore bright red arm bands and bright red headbands, and their remarks were openly Marxist. Several people were selling a tabloid paper called *Socialist Voice*. A large number of the placards bore the initials *RWL* which I discovered means Revolutionary Workers' League. There was no doubt about it, socialism was there in force in Canada, and we discerned a growing Marxist-Leninist orientation among people supporting the "gay rights" cause there.

The *Edmonton Sunday Sun* carried headlines that read: CAST OFF THOSE CHAINS THAT BIND and told of an incident which was as graphic a demonstration as any we've seen of what sin will do to an individual. The police had come to us prior to the beginning of a concert to report that a young man had bound himself by the neck with a heavy chain to a railing in the coliseum. The police offered to get torches and cut him loose. I looked up and saw the photographers ready, waiting for pictures of the police dragging this "poor man" out. I told the police I could not tell them what to do, but I gave them the benefit of some of our previous experiences and ended by saying, "If it were me, I'd leave him there and let him rattle around. Everything the homosexuals have thrown at us, God has turned around and used for our good. You watch and see what God does with this." So they left the fellow alone.

When Anita started to sing, the protestor rattled his chains and yelled, "You have me in shackles, Anita."

Anita directed an "I love you," at him, and he yelled back, "You love me so much you want me in prison."

"No," Anita answered, "I love you enough to tell you the truth to keep you from eternal damnation."

Anita was standing under a banner which read: JESUS SAID, "YE SHALL KNOW THE TRUTH, AND THE TRUTH SHALL MAKE YOU FREE" (JOHN 8:32).

The protestor continued to rattle the chain.

Reverend Campbell stepped to the microphone and said: "The devil has overstepped himself tonight. People, if this is not a picture of what sin will do to soul, I don't know what it is! Every time those chains rattle, just remember that sin will keep you in chains, sin will keep you in bondage, and only Jesus Christ can liberate, break those chains, and set you free."

The rattle of the chains wasn't heard again! He realized from that point on that everything he said or did was going to be counterproductive.

We believe it was much more than mere coincidence that upon our return home from that trip, there was a note from a dear friend calling our attention to Psalms 68:6: "God setteth the solitary in families: he bringeth out those which are bound with chains . . . ." This friend had no way of knowing what had happened in Canada!

In the book *The Returns of Love,* the young pseudonymous author reveals his struggle in learning to face and control his homosexual tendency and in so doing provides an answer to the question, Are we headed for enlightenment or deterioration? He points to Christ and says, "The sympathetic Christ, in all points tempted like as we are . . . expects us to resist to the limit.

"And one does suffer. A crucified passion, like a crucified man, is a long time dying, and it dies hard and painfully. But crucified it must be. As Paul says, 'those who belong to Christ Jesus have crucified the flesh with its passions and desires,' and I've had to learn to do just that. The 'flesh' revives often enough, and from its cross cries out for something to satisfy it: 'I thirst.' Then *let* it thirst. Old-fashioned Christian morality may sometimes be an agonizing way, it it is my way.

"I feel I'm a child in these matters, and I'm glad I am, because like a child I need the security of a moral framework, and like a child I need a standard of right and wrong. Give me the magnetic needle that says 'This is North,' or the law of gravity that says 'This is Down,' and then I know where I am. Show me the scripture that says, 'This is Sin,' and then I know where I am; and though the temptation to the sin in question may tear my heart in two, by the grace of God I *will* not transgress that law."

Anita and I are committed to getting both the Christian and the secular world to confront the truth. This resolve was reinforced at an Easter service in Miami Marine Stadium where Anita participated in the sunrise service with Charles Colson (*Born Again* author). We spent a beautiful day with Chuck and his wife, Patty, after which he sent a long letter and an enclosure:

> I am enclosing a letter which John Wesley wrote from his deathbed to William Wilberforce. It inspired Wilberforce for a twenty year crusade. I hope it will inspire you as it does me . . . . His life, I believe, is a model for people like you and me and an incredible testimony to what God can do with a man or woman fully committed to Him . . . .

The enclosure to which Chuck Colson referred was the last letter
Wesley wrote which reads:

My dear Sir,
   Unless the Divine Power has raised you up to be as
Athanasius, *contra mundum,* I see not how you can go
through your glorious enterprise in opposing that execrable
villainy which is the scandal of religion, of England, and of
human nature. Unless God has raised you up for this very
thing, you will be worn out by the opposition of men and
devils; but *if God be for you, who can be against you?* Are all
of them together stronger than God? Oh, *be not weary in well
doing.* Go on, in the name of God and in the power of His
might, till even American slavery, the vilest that ever saw the
sun, shall vanish away before it . . . .
   That He who has guided you from your youth up, may
continue to strengthen you in this and in all things, is the
prayer of,

Dear Sir,
Your affectionate servant,
John Wesley

We were marvelously encouraged by the letter and enclosure
from Charles Colson. "We felt a great spiritual kinship with both
of you. We admire your courage enormously. We are grateful to
God that He has raised you up 'for such a time as this' . . . ."
   Colson told the Easter worshipers: "Jesus Christ offers us the
way to live with ourselves, the way to live with God, the way to
live with our neighbors, and the way to live with society."
   Anita and I can do no more than to continue to echo that
refrain. In so doing, we are asking God to enlighten the church as
it stands firm on its God-given biblical authority.

11
A Cancer on the Soul
of Society

> . . . love in classic Greece was peculiarly, and even
> startlingly, different in character from later and con-
> temporary Western conceptions of love. For it was
> considered not so much an enobling and transforming
> goal of life, but an amusing pastime and distraction
> . . . And heartfelt expressions were poured forth not
> by young men and women who desired each other as
> mates, but by married men serenading their courte-
> sans, and by homosexuals (or lesbians) wooing others
> of their kind.
>
> MORTON M. HUNT
> *The Natural History of Love*

If those members of society who find nothing wrong with practicing homosexuals will not accept the biblical standard, then let
them look at the history of ancient Greece and Rome. It is a
dreadfully grim picture that emerges, a "catalogue of imperial
perversion," where society from the highest to the lowest was
equally affected. One thing is certain—the citizens of ancient
Greece and Rome were not exemplars of morality.

Historians, sociologists, and theologians have been warning for
many years that the parallel between ancient Greece and Rome
and what is happening in America today gives every indication

121

that we are headed on a collision course with moral disaster. Because I have read that and heard it stated so many times, I decided to do some investigating on my own. As I have read and researched this subject, I have discovered that all historians emphasize that disciplined control builds up civilized societies and where this discipline is scorned and refused, the breakdown of society is imminent. And this is what we are facing in America today. I am not an historian nor even a very astute student of history, but I have read enough to make me understand that we in this country are at a crossroads—either we return to the kind of biblical morality which God has set before us, or we continue on the downward course which the godless secular world is trying to enforce upon us.

It has been suggested that to look into the culture of Greece and Rome is to engage upon a hazardous kind of historical television! As it pertains to the subject of homosexuality, what is revealed from the archeologists' discoveries in centuries-old ruins and writings from antiquity is rampant immorality, promiscuity, and sexual license. Harlotry was a well-plied profession with many specialities. There were common brothels where the girls allowed their prospective purchasers to examine them like dogs in a kennel. No stigma seemingly was attached to married or unmarried men patronizing the courtesans, and many of them achieved a certain immortality through literature as they plied their "trade."

But what was a shocking discovery for me was the fact that while these girls and women had men contending for their favors, their chief rivals were the boys and men. I was amazed when I discovered that the love lyrics which are so frequently quoted and held up in such romantic light were in most instances written by men to other men or boys. Many of these men were married and were equally attracted by both sexes. One Greek statesman, Demosthenes, explained to a jury in one sentence: "Mistresses we keep for pleasure, concubines for daily attendance upon our persons, and wives to bear us legitimate children and be our housekeepers." Greek men, for the most part, found the wedded state distasteful; it was expensive, bothersome, and a hindrance to their personal freedom. One of the ancient sixth-century-B.C. lawmakers, it is claimed, passed a law making marriage compulsory because it had become so unpopular that the ongoing of the state itself was endangered. The Greek poet Palladas summed up the way men regarded marriage in this cruel epigram:

Marriage brings a man only two happy days: The day he takes his bride to bed, and the day he lays her in her grave.

Antifeminism has roots in Greece. Greek men have been considered passionate lovers traditionally, but much of their lovemaking was spent in homosexual relations. Because of this, the brothels became hothouses of Lesbian romance with the women turning to other women to satisfy their urges.

The very name *Lesbian* traces its origin to the Greek island of Lesbos where the homosexual woman Sappho ran a sort of finishing school for girls. This woman wrote a great deal of poetry (5 percent of it survived the later book burning by Christian zealots), which has had an immense influence on subsequent erotic literature. She penned in sensuous poems her lovesickness for the girls who attended her school.

Greek women rebelled in their own way at the treatment that was being accorded them by men. They began to participate actively in the cultural pursuits of the time and made many significant contributions to letters, science, philosophy, and art. Will Durant in his monumental work *The Life of Greece* (*The Story of Civilization: Part 2*) explains that the partial emancipation of women was accompanied by a revolt against wholesale maternity, and the limitation of the family became the outstanding social phenomenon of the age.

As I reflected on the demands of Lesbians and women in the radical women's movements of today and studied the statistics on abortions, I saw a parallel to what happened in ancient Greece.

It is now common knowledge, particularly since the five-million-dollar fiasco called erroneously the National Women's Convention held in Houston in November 1977, that this federally funded IWY (International Women's Year) Conference was run by a political powerhouse within the "feminist" movement largely comprised of Lesbians. "Straight" women at the state conventions which preceded the Houston monstrosity, as well as at the Houston event, were subjected to Lesbian outrages so bad that they could not even be described in full in the *Congressional Record*. This was clearly not a representation of normal American womanhood. Those who attended and were in a position to assess the entire revolting event where obscene slogans and Lesbian sex gadgets were hawked everywhere, reported it was anti-male, antiwhite, antifamily, anti-Christian, and anti-American from start to finish.

One of the more tragic aspects of the conference was the presence of two former first ladies—Betty Ford and Lady Bird Johnson—and our present first lady, Rosalyn Carter. The conference was in actuality a "media event" staged for the benefit of media coverage with the presence of these three women planned to lend dignity to an otherwise rigged series of sessions merely following a scenario that was prescripted long in advance.

What happened in Houston proved that these revolutionary women have one aim: destroy the social structure on which America rests. The women's movement is making an intensive effort to promote abortion, the ERA, and privileges enabling homosexuals and Lesbians to teach in our schools, to rent from any landlord, and to have custody of children. These are but a few of their aims and were included in resolutions passed in Houston.

In contrast was the well-ordered Pro-Family Rally held at the Astro-Arena in Houston at the same time. Some 20,000 people assembled, coming from every state in the Union. It was an enthusiastic crowd which was largely ignored by the media. I wanted very much to attend, but we had a long-standing previous booking. I did send a filmed greeting which was shown. What this countermeeting proved was that the "feminist" movement is facing a strong, well-organized grass-roots opposition which is zealous in its fight against ERA, and all that is regarded as a threat to family life. This country has not heard the end of these women, many of them dedicated Christians, and the consequences for the women's liberation movement and the hysterical Houston "feminists" will be seen and felt.

I personally took it upon myself, at the time of our entrance into the Dade County battle with the militant homosexuals, to write our legislators and commissioners and urge them to vote no on the (then) upcoming so-called Equal Rights Amendment referendum. As it developed, it was defeated in Florida.

I am greatly concerned about militant Lesbians and their avowed plan to obtain their "rights" in the teaching profession. Jean O'Leary, co-executive director of the National Gay Task Force, was appointed by President Carter to serve on the National Commission for the Observance of International Women's Year. She has gone on record as laying out a strategy that will give "students and faculty the right to acknowledge their Lesbian identities openly and seek out intelligent information about themselves."

In her plan to end what she calls the "oppression of Lesbians" she is demanding that changes be made in the following areas:

Counseling. School counselors should "be required to take courses on human sexuality in which a comprehensive and positive view of Lesbianism is presented. Lesbians as well as heterosexual counselors should be represented on the guidance staff."

Not content with this only, she wants the names and the phone numbers of gay counseling services to be made available to all students and school psychologists.

"No school counselor should ever refer a student to a psychotherapist for the purpose of changing her/his sexual preference from 'gay' to straight . . . ."

Sex Education Courses. These are to be taught by persons

who have taken the human-sexuality courses already mentioned. And students should be encouraged "to explore alternate life-styles, including Lesbianism." Moreover, "speakers from local Lesbian organizations should be invited to these classes so that students can have their questions answered firsthand."

The plan would do away with all textbooks which do not mention Lesbianism favorably or refer to it as a mental disorder. "Positive views of Lesbianism" are to be taught in our schools.

Lesbian Studies and Lesbian Clubs. These should be set up to "foster pride in the adolescent Lesbian . . . and a community spirit among Lesbians . . . ."

Libraries. Bibliographies of Lesbian literature and novels, stories, poetry, and nonfiction books portraying the "joy of women loving women," are to be supplied in school libraries and "the use of these books should be encouraged in literature and history classes."

I cannot urge readers strongly enough to be aware of these demands and to guard carefully your own local educational institutions against inroads by flaunting and militant Lesbians and homosexuals whose motives are subject to question. In a *Vogue* magazine article (August 1977), writer Anne Roiphe asks the question: "Who's Afraid of Lesbian Sex?" and answers it by stating: "Unknown to parents who were paying for education they expected to result in socially acceptable marriages and conventional fulfillments, the actual teaching by Lesbian women, while in no way sexual (hardly ever was a student seduced by an older woman), was in many ways totally subversive . . . ."

One of the heart-wrenching letters in our possession comes from a now happily married Christian woman who missed out on a satisfying emotional relationship with her mother in her preteenage years. In her constant search for the right mother image, she developed a friendship with one of her teachers that became a wretched Lesbian relationship. "I desperately wanted out. I begged and pleaded with her to no avail . . . she retaliated with threats . . . it became emotional blackmail . . . ."

Who says homosexuals and Lesbians, flaunting their perverted sexuality, aren't a potential danger to our children? We have *many* similar letters on file. We also have *many* news clippings showing cases of homosexual teachers who have been convicted of sex charges and similar documented cases of scout and other club leaders. One of the most shocking incidents is that of four homosexuals charged with murdering a twelve-year-old boy in Toronto on July 29, 1977. Yes, murders by heterosexuals occur and with even more frequency (because according to available statistics there are more heterosexuals than homosexuals), but this does not diminish the danger nor the reality of homosexual molestation and murder. According to *Time* magazine (July 18, 1977), the two biggest mass murders in the history of our country were perpetrated by homosexuals in Texas and California.

Some homosexuals are known to go into jealous rages. The potential danger to our children exists. As I researched the subject, I discovered that mature men in ancient Greece felt that the ideal love relationship was that between an older man and a youth. Plutarch tells of a tall and handsome youth in Athens who was always accompanied by a swarm of men who courted and flattered him as though he were a beautiful girl. The youth became an expert at taunting, flirting, and frustrating his lovers, and allowing homosexual favors when it pleased or profited him. Morton M. Hunt (*The Natural History of Love*) labeled him "an insolent hero."

Interestingly, Hunt says that however romantic the lover's conduct, or complete his success in the wooing, the relationship usually disintegrated when the lad's beard was fully grown!

Aristotle, in his writings, frowned on actual homosexual coition and called it a "morbid abnormality." Plato, who wrote ecstatically of boy love in his early dialogues, in his later years changed his mind and condemned homosexual contact altogether as being contrary to nature and productive of intemperate habits and ef-feminacy. Socrates, the Athenian idealist philosopher and teacher, wrote of boy love. The literary evidence is overwhelm-ingly clear—emotional liaisons among men and boys were the fashion. All of which reinforces in my own thinking that present-day practicing homosexuals prefer the younger boy (and what better place to find one than in our schools?).

Another less commonly used name for these relationships is *pederasty*. Even though Greek homosexuality was almost univer-sally practiced, it had bad connotations even in that immoral society and was considered abnormal. And it was *never* legalized. Because of the bad connotations, the Greeks tried to intimate by the choice of the word *pederasty* a relationship which was closer and more intimate than that between even a father and a son.

Greek men rationalized that love for a youth who had physical and intellectual appeal improved the character of both lover and beloved. It is amazing to what extent the sinful heart will go to justify its wickedness.

But why did homosexuality, including pederasty, flourish as it did in Greece? It is a question that needs to be asked and an-swered, and the explanation substantiates our concern that we must protect America's children from the same fate as the Greek youth. For you see, the real center of homosexuality in Greece lay in its education system. Educationally the home was often deficient, and fathers and mothers were too busy to look after the total welfare of their own sons and daughters. (If that doesn't sound like the situation in *this* country, I don't know what does!) A youth in Greece, therefore, attached himself to a man, and while the relationship may have begun with lofty ideals, it more often than not degenerated into a thoroughly carnal relationship. Greek education was homosexual through and through. Today's homosexuals and Lesbians cry, "We must provide role models," a false plea which has overtones harking back to the corruption which ancient Greece experienced.

Much of this perversion can be traced back to the gymnastic

training which became so typical of Greek education. The athletic prowess of Greek athletes is generally known and acknowledged. There is scarcely a sport at which they did not excel. The real religion of the Greeks was the worship of health, beauty, and strength. Ancient war depended upon the physical vigor and skill of its warriors. The men had to fight to defend their soil. History tells of the brave exploits of Greek men in war. This was said to result from homosexual pairing of the men in battles where both lover and youth would rather die than act cowardly in each other's sight. This was considered a military asset!

Greek games were Panhellenic—involving all their peoples. The splendor and popularity of athletics in Greece can be seen yet today in our regard for Olympic games. It was in Olympia where the greatest contests of all were held. But it was the gymnasium with its emphasis on physical training and nudity which, according to almost all Greek writers, saw the beginning of the lust of men for boys. Ennius, an old Latin writer, said, "It is the beginning of vice to bare the body among citizens." And Plato emphasized, "Pederasty is the price paid for the nude gymnasia." No wonder the Apostle Paul came along and said:

Wherefore God also gave them up to uncleanness through the lusts of their own hearts, to dishonour their own bodies between themselves: Who changed the truth of God into a lie, and worshipped and served the creature more than the Creator, who is blessed for ever. Amen. For this cause God gave them up unto vile affections [passions]: for even their women did change the natural use into that which is against nature: And likewise also the men, leaving the natural use of the woman, burned in their lust one toward another; men with men working that which is unseemly, and receiving in themselves that recompence of their error which was meet. And even as they did not like to retain God in their knowledge, God gave them over to a reprobate mind, to do those things which are not convenient [fitting].

Romans 1:24–28

It should come as no surprise that Paul's preaching was no-where laughed at and scorned so much as it was by the Athenians. Is it any wonder the depraved men and women who proudly call themselves "gay" have lashed out at me so strongly? The com-mentator Matthew Henry makes the observation, "A man cannot be delivered up to a greater slavery than to be given up to his own lusts." The blind understanding of the homosexual and Lesbian is caused by their own willful aversion. They can never say they have not had the truth of God's Word shown to them. The Bible constantly warns of the danger of sinning when one has heard the truth (*see* James 4:17).

The Bible is in agreement with secular history; both of which faithfully record the divine judgment which fell upon those once-great civilizations of Greece and Rome. This is the world into which Christianity came with its emphasis on moral living. God was giving these people every opportunity to repent of their sins, to turn to Him and change their ways. That same opportunity is being offered to sinners today regardless whether their "sin" is homosexuality or any other willful disregard of what God has plainly set before us in the Bible as the standard by which we are to live.

I think it is terribly important that we understand the background of all this so that we can more easily comprehend why Paul was so emphatic in what he said. This also explains why I have so consistently referred to these Scripture verses. Until we became involved in the Dade County homosexual issue—an issue which, by the way, we always remind the media, and now you, the reader, that *they* brought to the forefront of public thinking—I had not bothered to inform myself, nor had I heard much preach-ing in churches setting forth the degeneracy into which the Greek and Roman worlds had fallen.

I read that the ancient writer Plutarch, among others, finally was horrified at what he saw taking place. Believe me, my own horror was no less than his! As we observe those in the homosexual community seeking to impose upon our society legislation which would grant them special privileges and make it possible for them to gain accessibility to our educational systems, carrying with them their outrageous demands (and rights, if the laws are eventually passed), I am appalled that our lawmakers, who should know what happened in ancient cultures, would take such a tolerant attitude. Some of them, in fact, are responsible for introducing such legislation and working hard to see it made into law. I think, for instance, of Mayor Ed Koch of New York City who undermines and undercuts New York State's antisodomy laws and endorses and encourages homosexuality and homosexuals in everything he does. He has gone on record as stating: "This is one mayor who will not be intimidated by the people of this city," making it obvious that he will not be guided by the people who elected him. And he is not alone!

The real danger of ERA and special-privilege laws passed on local levels is that they will in the final analysis be enforced by local judges. How many judges are there throughout the land who are like the judge in Santa Fe, New Mexico, who ruled that a woman of twenty-three, by engaging in sexual intercourse with a boy of fifteen, had contributed to his worldly education—not his delinquency? The judge stated: "The legislature has abolished fornication as a crime. In doing so, it cast aside the ancient religious doctrine that forbids such practices. It recognized, as a matter of public policy, that this conduct did not violate the mores of the twentieth century. Today, sexual intercourse is recognized as normal conduct in the development of a human being. As a result, this subject is taught to children in the public schools . . . ."

Columnist Patrick Buchanan, speaking in defense of the Supreme Court's decision to uphold the Tacoma, Washington, school system's firing of a homosexual teacher, wrote: "A teacher is not simply an instructor. He or she is also an example, a potential influence upon the child for life. Parents have a right not to have their children held in a captive audience, daily, before a teacher whose admitted life style is abhorrent—whether that individual be a professed homosexual or someone President Carter would characterize as 'living in sin' . . . .

"Despite the fire being directed at the court from civil liberties brigades, it ruled correctly . . . ."

But back to ancient writers. Plato, in one of his last books, *The Laws*, vehemently attacked homosexuality and wrote: "The intercourse of men with men, or of women with women is contrary to nature, and the bold attempt was originally due to unbridled lust. How can we take precautions against the unnatural loves of either sex, from which innumerable evils have come upon individuals and cities? How shall we devise a remedy and a way of escape out of so great a danger? We must abolish altogether the connection of men with men . . . . Who would ever think of establishing such a practice by law? Certainly no one who had in his mind the true image of law."

Those are serious questions Plato raised in his day. We need to raise them again today! How can *we* take precautions? We can through constant vigilance and a readiness to jump into the forefront of the fight to stop such laws from being enacted on local levels. That is what we did. That is what concerned Americans—whether you call yourself Christian or not—are going to have to continue to do. And not just over the matter of militant homosexuals, but on all issues that threaten our nation's families.

And what about Rome? Rome fared no better. In fact, homosexuality in that city became even worse than it ever became in Greece. The Romans conquered Greece, but then Rome itself was conquered morally by the very ones she had defeated. Homosexuality finally had such a grip on Roman society that, as the historian Gibbon reminds the reader, fourteen out of the first fifteen emperors were practicing homosexuals. Very few today would know that the "great Caesar" was a perfumed homosexual; however, his sexual indulgences were not confined to men as history has shown. Romans called him "the husband of every woman and the wife of every man," which gives some indication of multiple liaisons.

We must note, however, that as saturated with sick sex as Roman society was, and as obsessed as her rulers were with perverted practices (particularly on boys), in Rome, as in Greece, homosexuality was *never* legalized.

I have been greatly helped by reading William Barclay's book *The Ten Commandments for Today* in which he presents timeless truths for today's moral issues. In this book he reminds the reader that the historian J. D. Unwin studied eighty-eight different civilizations, and from the study discerned the following pattern: "Every civilization is established and consolidated by observing a strict moral code, is maintained while this strict code is kept, and decays when sexual license is allowed . . . . Any human society is free to choose either to display great energy or to enjoy sexual freedom; the evidence is that it cannot do both for more than one generation." Barclay states: "It may well be that the lesson of history is that the loosening of sexual standards threatens the welfare of not only the individual, but also of the nation."

We need to heed the words of the writer of Proverbs: "Righteousness exalteth a nation: but sin is a reproach to any people" (Proverbs 14:34).

12

Homosexuality Did Not Come From the Womb

> Researchers have been searching for the chromosomal proof for homosexuality for almost half a century. They have yet to find it.
>
> But the homosexual apologists keep right on looking and keep on talking as if the proof already exists.
>
> Debates about the cause of homosexuality continue, even among those sympathetic to the gays. About the only thing they can agree on among themselves is that the Bible is wrong on the subject, while man in his "superior wisdom" and secular mercy just has to be right.
>
> WILLIAM D. RODGERS
> *The Gay Invasion*

When homosexuals are asked, as they frequently are on radio and TV talk shows, "When did you become homosexual?" they tell you at what age approximately they had decided to become "gay." Anita and I find that very enlightening, for it dispels the myth that homosexuals were born that way since we have no way of deciding when to become heterosexual.

We also find it interesting that homosexuals say they do not molest children, yet when questioned as to their first homosexual experience, most of them state their first encounter was as a child with a friend of the family, a relative, an older teenager, a neighbor, or adult acquaintance. Rarely is this first experience reported, for the child is fearful to tell his parents.

We have letters and have had numerous conversations with students who readily admit they generally know it when a teacher is homosexual. The teacher may not be teaching or openly advocating homosexuality, but the students easily pick up on attitudes and are more observant and knowledgeable than we often give them credit for.

The more we read, and the more we see and observe the lifestyle of homosexuals, the more we are convinced that homosexuality did not come from the womb. You will never find God creating or championing the unnatural, and homosexuality is against nature.

In the previously mentioned book *Is the Homosexual My Neighbor?*, the authors go to extremes to try and explain away the Romans 1 passage which deals with the unnaturalness of homosexual practices. In the efforts of those who would defend homosexuality, there is a watering down of the revealed will of God, that is after an individual has heard the truth, a putting away of sin is required. Bennett J. Sims, writing in *Christianity Today* (February 24, 1978), states: "I cannot escape the conclusion that homosexual behavior is explicitly and implicitly regarded as deviate and sinful especially in light of Romans 1." It is the belief of theologians that "no adequate Christian position on homosexuality can be taken without regard for the Bible as a decisive norm." Sims repeatedly emphasizes that in the Bible heterosexual sex is clearly affirmed as God's will for humanity, that which is natural and right according to the plan of the Creator. There are those who argue that homosexual love is as lofty as the best heterosexual sex relationship. You cannot find one instance in the Word of God that says anything good about homosexuality; in every instance where it is mentioned it is condemned.

There are those who argue that when homosexuality is practiced in the motivating context of love, it is not sinful or wrong and that such as these are exempt from the Apostle Paul's condemnation of the act. To carry this argument to its logical conclusion we would have to say there are loving ways to murder, malign people, to hate, and do other things which the Bible expressly warns as being contrary to the will of God. Sims says it better than I. "This is moral absurdity."

There are those who are quick to point out that Jesus in the New Testament doesn't speak of homosexuality. Let us be equally quick to point out that Jesus' teachings with respect to marriage are clearly stated. Heterosexual love is shown to be God's will and therefore good and normal. Jesus spoke very plainly about fornication, and homosexuals cannot escape Jesus' judgment against sexual sin.

"Those who belong to Christ have nailed their natural evil desires to his cross and crucified them there" (Galatians 5:24 LB). We have hundreds of letters which demonstrate that when an individual truly abandons his sinful bent (regardless of what that is, but including homosexuality), the power of the crucified and risen Christ is there to help such a person rid himself of the old sin nature.

The Apostle Paul reminds readers that we have been given freedom in Christ, but *not* freedom to do wrong.

I advise you to obey only the Holy Spirit's instructions. He will tell you where to go and what to do, and then you won't always be doing the wrong things your evil nature wants you to. For we naturally love to do evil things that are just the opposite from the things that the Holy Spirit tells us to do; and the good things we want to do when the Spirit has his way with us are just the opposite of our natural desires. These two forces within us are constantly fighting each other to win control over us, and our wishes are never free from their pressures.

Galatians 5:16, 17 LB

The question is posed by Scanzoni and Mollenkott that when a homosexual person loves Jesus Christ and wants "above all to acknowledge God in all of life, yet for some unknown reasons feels drawn to someone of the same sex, for the sake of love rather than lust," is it then "fair to describe that person as lustful or desirous of forgetting God's existence?" The Bible supplies the answer. "Let no man say when he is tempted, I am tempted of God: for God cannot be tempted with evil, neither tempteth he any man: But every man is tempted, when he is drawn away of his own lust, and enticed" (James 1:13, 14).

The "unknown reason" mentioned above is *sin,* specifically *lust.* Let us call it by its rightful name. That same passage says when lust is conceived (acted upon), it leads to the death penalty from God.

Both Anita and I, as parents, have sat with letters in our hands from grieving parents of daughters who have chosen Lesbian life-styles and sons who have opted for homosexuality, and we have joined parents such as these in grief. Anita has been asked, "What if, despite your efforts, one of your kids turned out to be a homosexual? Would you disown him or her?"

She expresses the way we both feel when she says, "I would never disown my children, no matter what." Anita and I believe in demonstrating our love to our children. Not a day goes by in which we fail to grab our kids, roughhouse with them, or hold them tenderly and say, "I love you." Anita has a real thing about this. If she feels that she is failing as a mother to her children, then she feels she will have failed completely. I join her in these feelings. If I am a failure as a father, then I am a first-class failure. Our children are our first priority, regardless how busy we may be in other pursuits.

If, God forbid, one of our kids chose the homosexual life-style, we would sit down and explain to him or her that he's hurting no one but himself and that God cannot tolerate that kind of sin. Its consequences will be tragic. We would tell the child that true happiness eludes those who rebel against the revealed will of God and choose the way of sin rather than God's way.

If one of our kids chose to rebel against God by living a life-style that embraced any activity which the Bible clearly labels sin, we would be equally quick to point out to that child the consequences.

That's why we identify with grieving parents. We would grieve too if this happened with one of our children. One mother wrote expressing how she was going through her "own particular brand of hell." She told of the beautiful relationship she and her daughter had always enjoyed. Then she related how a course in human sexuality and feminism in college changed her daughter. "She used to chide me about the terms I used, antiquated to her new-found knowledge, to denote women's place in society. I mean women were *women*, not girls, or ladies, or any other colloquial phrases. She soon discovered in a six-week course that *my* whole language structure, as well as that of the world, was archaic."

She said her daughter developed a strong emotional relationship with a fellow student, a divorced woman with children, and the pair began traveling together. It was then discovered that the two had a Lesbian relationship. "My shock was so profound that initially I went to pieces, but begged her to let me help her. She agreed to see some counselors, one of which was our pastor from whom she received no help. We sought sex therapists who advised *me* to accept her behavior. She claimed to be happy, and didn't I want her to be happy?

"We have gone everywhere from other counselors to psychologists to psychiatrists—all offer the same suggestion, 'Accept it, it's a way of life.' " This woman sadly commented, "I know it's a way of life, but a sinful way, and I am now ready to fight to help my daughter realize what she is doing . . . . *I cannot let her die until she comes back to God.*" This mother offered her services to Protect America's Children to help bring sons and daughters of other parents out of this kind of bondage to sin and back into clean moral living.

A letter from a psychiatrist states: "Psychiatrists are supposed to be mighty liberal when it comes to acceptance of homosexuality, but the above letterhead labels a man who is *not* one of them. I say sodomy is sodomy, and there are no 'degrees,' no 'exceptions.' The results of their life-style pay a lot of the bills around here and I salute you. I feel you have given the nation a huge gift with your stand, even if some of its citizens don't realize it yet. We will continue to pray for you in this heavy issue . . . ."

A 1972 study of homosexuals by Masters and Johnson, the premier sexologists of our time, revealed that 43 percent of the homosexuals interviewed had their first homosexual experiences before they were twelve years old. Kinsey has provided sobering evidence that such initial experiences are very often permanently damaging. Another group of psychologists bluntly stated recently that "Heterosexuality is the biologic norm and unless interfered with, all individuals are heterosexual." Kinsey's 1950 research findings conclude that there is no data which proves the existence of hormonal factors indicating that specific hereditary factors are involved. There is mounting evidence that homosexuality did not come from the womb.

To blame parents for the moral failure in their children's lives is a blanket indictment which is both unfair and unwise. Parents are going to feel that they are failures anyway without friends, relatives, and judgmental society censuring them. To be sure, there *are* parents who have contributed to moral delinquency in the lives of their offspring, but that blame cannot be laid at the feet of *all* parents whose children make a deliberate choice to go against nature. Homosexuals who think they themselves suffer should also consider the pain and grief this brings to their parents. There are stereotypes attached to parents, too, which are not totally justified: the cold, rejecting father; the dominating, overbearing mother. Careful researchers have demonstrated that these labels do not necessarily apply to all parents of homosexual individuals. At one point I do agree with Scanzoni and Mollenkott, and that is their statement, "Parents of homosexual persons often suffer great anguish because they have been led to believe they are to blame for their children's sexual orientation."

The next time you are tempted to blame parents, think twice before heaping that kind of guilt upon already suffering mothers and fathers. Can you imagine the suffering endured by the mother who wrote telling of her son's "sexual reassignment"? Or the heartache of that mother who describes the feelings that swept over her when she learned her youngest son was a homosexual? She calls it "a tragedy." "This twenty-two-year-old young man is very handsome, not at all the limp-wristed, high-pitched-voice, swishy-type boy. We thought we had an average, wholesome, all-American family of three children . . . . He even married a beautiful, sweet Christian girl and they have a lovable, adorable baby girl . . . . The word 'gay' is a misnomer for he is the most unhappy, miserable person alive. The sad, hurt look in his eyes tears at our heartstrings . . . . His wife has divorced him . . . . But our love has not lessened for him; it has grown. We will take a homosexual son rather than a dead one . . . ."

Among the many testimonies and letters we have from those who once considered themselves to be homosexual, I found this statement:

Are some people born gay?
I believe not.

It may appear to some of us that we have always been that way; but I know now that God would not create someone contradictory to His desire.

What brought each of us to the "gay" life could be a lot of different things.

What is important is what we do about it.

There may be some "gays" reading this who can't comprehend enjoying life with the opposite sex, but don't sell God short. He can do anything *if only you let Him.* Remember, He only has good things in mind for us if only we will trust Him. God will not violate your personality, but *He will clean out those old wrong ideas that we have talked ourselves into believing over the years,* and He will make you the best you can be.

God is not a liar. He promises that if we confess our sinfulness, turn ourselves over to Him, love Him and do as He leads and tells us to do in the Bible, that He *will* handle all the circumstances and repercussions.

Notice this individual's comment: *He will clean out those old wrong ideas that we have talked ourselves into believing over the years.* That has to be very significant. Another former homosexual quoted in *Light and Life* magazine said: "I was homosexually oriented for over twenty years of my life. I have traveled the tangled trail of homosexuality from the beginning to the gates of suicide—and back again. *I know how I came to be gay, and I know how I became free.*" This writer asserts that the undeniable chaos of his life as a homosexual proves beyond contradiction that the "gay" life was (and is) sinful, unproductive, noncreative, and depersonalizing. He emphasizes, "A more emphatic indictment of any style of living cannot be made. Any life pattern, straight or 'gay,' which offers suicide as an escape is truly a tragic life. We do not need to condemn homosexuality. The 'gay' lifestyle stands self-condemned."

This same writer insists, "When God comes into the life of a sinner, gives him new life, and begins a change process, this change always occurs by displacement." He explains that to mean "to get rid of darkness, we do not mess with the darkness." The Bible reinforces this:

This then is the message which we have heard of him, and declare unto you, that God is light, and in him is no darkness at all. If we say that we have fellowship with him, and walk in darkness, we lie, and do not the truth: But if we walk in the light, as he is in the light, we have fellowship one with another, and the blood of Jesus Christ his Son cleanseth us from all sin. If we say that we have no sin, we deceive ourselves, and the truth is not in us. If we confess our sins, he is faithful and just to forgive us our sins, and to cleanse us from all unrighteousness. If we say that we have not sinned, we make him a liar, and his word is not in us.

1 John 1:5–10

He continued, "The way out of the homosexual prison is simple, sure, and speedy. And for anyone who wants out, really wants out, the odds are one hundred to nothing in his favor. He can begin his journey to freedom any time he wants. How?

"First, determine the evidence for the existence of God . . . .

"Trust the Scripture. In those places where you do not understand or where you find seeming contradictions, assign the error to your own comprehension, not to the Bible. After all, if you knew the truth, you would already be free.

"Commit yourself to know the truth, and focus your attention and energy there. Satan will keep dragging your mind back to the problem if he can . . . . Satan is a liar and has been so from the beginning . . . ."

Truth displaces deception as the individual allows the Holy Spirit to minister and confirm truth in his mind. A transformation is assured as the Holy Spirit undertakes to do for the person what he cannot do for himself. The Holy Spirit is a teacher and directs our attention to areas of our mind that need renewal. Whether we are homosexually inclined or are struggling with other sin bents, the process is the same. When we confess known sin, accept God's forgiveness, stand on the truths we are learning, and then put into practice and obey and yield, we will experience the truth of John 8:32: "And ye shall know the truth, and the truth shall make you free."

Two ex-homosexuals working with an organization called EXIT (EX-gay Intervention Team), based at the Melodyland Hotline Center, Anaheim, California, were quoted in the *Ventura County Star-Free Press* as saying that the major reason for leaving homosexuality is to be consistent with what God teaches.

"Gayness is learned. It can be unlearned. It is not true 'once gay, always gay,' " they say.

The large number of testimonies such as these leaves no doubt in our minds that homosexuality did not come from the womb and that there is hope for the homosexual. Anita and I stand prepared to help those who want help.

Anita and Bob

13
The Future

> The righteous is a guide to his neighbor, But the way of
> the wicked leads them astray.
>
> Proverbs 12:26 NAS

Anita Sums Up . . .

We are living in the midst of a social revolution in our society.
My heart's cry is wake up, wake up America, before it's too late.

From all over the country, however, there is mounting evidence that citizens are being awakened and awareness is coming
upon more and more people that we are living in turbulent times
and that we do not intend to stand by idly and let this country go
down in moral ruin. Bob and I believe we have felt the heartbeat
of America; if we are wrong, then 80 percent of the American
people are wrong. The majority of the American people are fun-
damentally good—perhaps just not as vocal as the more militant
minority.

During 1978, among the many trips and events that stand out,
was the experience of speaking to the Oklahoma Senate. It was
state Senator Mary Helm who initiated the invitation. She is the
author of a bill which allows school boards to fire teachers who
advocate homosexual activity or engage in "public homosexual
activity." The bill won overwhelming approval in the Oklahoma
House. The "gay" activists were on the capitol steps, but did not
gain admission. It was my first speech before a legislative body,

145

and it was both humbling and thrilling. I told the senators I could hardly believe a little gal born in Barnsdall, Oklahoma, could be standing there. I jokingly told them, "I've thought about running for president, but changed my mind when I realized my husband would be the first lady." I reminded them, just as I do you, the reader, now, that people are crying out for moral men and women to be elected to state and national offices. When Bob and I talk about the future of this nation and the welfare of its citizens, we find ourselves almost in unison saying, "O God, give us right-thinking leaders, men and women who are committed to uphold-ing Bible standards of morality, who remember how this nation was founded, and are committed to its preservation."

In the months ahead, as the demands of the militant homosexu-als become even more strident in local and state-level elections, as the American people are forced to confront the issue in *all* its ramifications, and as more stark horror and violence are exposed, we believe the majority of Americans (who are deeply concerned about their families and their children) are going to recoil against homosexuality and its supporters. Even as this book is in its final stages of writing, newspapers are carrying accounts of a "Gay celebration" parade in Hollywood, California, where California's "gay" community is gearing itself for a fight against an initiative which will come before California voters in November, and if passed, will bar self-announced "gays" from teaching school in California.

Bob and I are familiar with these parades and demonstrations. It has been very disturbing on many occasions as in New York where the marching demonstrators hoisted above their heads a dummy of me burning in effigy.

I have been tremendously helped on such occasions by remem-bering accounts from the Bible of God's people and how they reacted in times of difficulty. "And David was greatly distressed; for the people spoke of stoning him . . . but David encouraged himself in the Lord his God" (1 Samuel 30:6).

In June 1978, homosexuals were making a travesty of even

scriptural terminology in announcing a "Reborn-Again-Loving People" rally marking the first anniversary since the repeal of what they called "human rights" in Dade County, "plus the beginning of all local and national energies being mobilized to counter an onslaught on the U.S. Constitution by the witch-hunt of Anita Bryant forces . . . ."

Their news sheet, widely circulated in Miami, urged readers that they "do anything but support the U.S. Constitution." A threat was made to expose politicians who "cater to Anita Bryant forces," and they announced their national campaign slogan as "Oral Is Moral." They boast that they expect to win in elections on "a whole range of issues from ERA; a comprehensive Bill of Rights tied into *all* local, state and federal funding; taxing the churches . . . ; sex education in schools; legalizing marijuana; legalizing prostitution . . . ." and other issues which sounds like a case of the inmates trying to take over the asylum.

Henry Steele Commager, in an article entitled "A Historian Looks at Our Political Morality" (*Commonweal* May 12, 1978), calls for a squaring of conduct with principles of law and morality. In that same magazine, Ralph C. Chandler, writing on the subject of ethics and public policy, makes the observation, "The historical record sustains the view that corruption is endemic in the American political system." This statement covers more than this nation's political system and is an accurate assessment of the overall plight of this nation. He adds that "our national history can be read as a litany of avarice and greed."

Vogue magazine in reporting on the new sexuality in its health column (August 1977), said: "Its primary purpose is gratification of carnal pleasure, and to _____ with the consequences, society, and morality."

A lawyer wrote us a letter in which he stated that nations have faltered and become nonexistent following a period of licentious and immoral conduct of the populace. "Homosexuality destroys the family unit and the fundamental strength of an existing society or nation is dependent upon the strong, healthy family unit or relationship. When the family-unit structure breaks down, then society or the nation composed of that society becomes decadent, depraved, despondent, disillusioned, and degenerated . . . . I know that homosexuals, historically, are aggressive in seeking out youths to become either the dominant or recessive sex partner, and secondly that the normal wife of the homosexual and mother of his children suffers a life of abomination.''

I am sure a vast number of Americans were revulsed when they heard news reports and read about the marine male-prostitute ring uncovered at Camp Pendleton, California, in July 1978. It had been operating for three years with its roots spreading into the Hollywood "gay" community some one hundred miles away. It was reported by an unnamed officer, "The recruiters looked for fair-skinned, young-looking kids and usually approached them on a one-to-one basis. They would strike up a conversation, eventually suggesting that good money could be made on weekends working for the ring." All twelve of the participating marines were discharged.

My concern is, what will happen to these young men as they go back into society? Who is attempting to reach out with help and hope to such as these?

Doctor Harold M. Voth, member of the staff at the Menninger Foundation and Associate Chief of Psychiatry for Education at the Topeka Veterans Hospital, states that the family unit faces peril in our country today. "Our land is being flooded by sick people with the coming of each generation. Our values are changing, our laws will change, and down we will go."

I found his analysis instructive. He calls attention to the emerging new ways of living which bear little resemblance to what characterized the American scene and our national character a few years ago. "Many great civilizations have collapsed at the very zenith of their growth . . . ." This knowledgeable man, and others like him, needs to be listened to. "The laws and traditions which have made us great will continue only if we as individuals within the land are strong and committed to upholding these traditions and values."

As I have listened to what he and others are saying, I see ominous signs that portend much future grief and anxiety for us as parents if we do not heed the warnings. With the Old Testament prophet I say, "O earth, earth, earth, hear the word of the Lord" (Jeremiah 22:29).

Bob Sums Up . . .

Award-winning editor and publisher Paul V. Osborne of the Decatur, Illinois, *Tribune* has gone on record as stating: "Attacking Anita Bryant has to be one of the most serious mistakes in judgment that any movement has made in this century!"

More than one columnist has observed that when a person turns his attention away from media events and their reporting, and from show-biz slurs, to get a reading of popular attitudes, an entirely different picture of Anita's standing in the eyes of the American people emerges.

In spite of the fact that there has been a rising crescendo of anti-Anita remarks, and that my wife has been vilified by homosexuals and homosexual supporters, to the credit of the silent-majority populace in this country, their thinking is reflected in some polls which cannot be disputed. One of the most publicized of these polls was *Good Housekeeping's* ninth annual Most Admired Women Poll. Readers cited Anita's courage, faith, and leadership among her most admirable qualities. Anita was a newcomer as a poll finalist coming out ahead of the wives of two former presidents and our present president. *Good Housekeeping* itself explained that readers went to great pains to spell out the reasons for selecting Anita, and their comments reflected great admiration and support.

I asked Anita for her reaction to this poll. "I know it represented grass-roots people, Bob. And I know, too, that it was not so much for me, Anita Bryant, that they were necessarily voting, as it was an opportunity for them to vocalize their own feelings of right and wrong. They were voicing suppressed feelings—finally someone had the courage to stand for her convictions regardless of the cost. This represented them; it was an opportunity to go on record that this is how they felt and let it be shown in a tangible way."

Another honor came her way when she was named to the "Twenty-five Most Influential Women in America" list for 1977. This list was compiled by a panel of prominent editors and social commentators for the *World Almanac & Book of Facts.*

Teenage beauty contestants from across the nation voted Anita "America's Greatest American." This contest was picketed by homosexual activists when they learned of the girls' choice.

There have been an incredible number of such awards and honors coming Anita's way. At first I thought of including more of them, but we saw the difficulty this presented—there are just too many of them. I noticed recently a simple tapestry hanging near Anita's desk which shows a single lovely rose. The tapesty reads: YOU HAVE TOUCHED ME—I HAVE GROWN. This is typical of the thoughtful gifts, awards, and honors she has received and which are so meaningful to her. Anita treasures each of them as representative of the love she has felt from countless thousands of concerned individuals. Because of this, she has felt *your* touch and God's, and Anita has truly grown.

Anita made a comment which has prompted us to take some big steps into the future. She said, "Bob, we need to tell the American people how much this has meant to us. Is there any adequate way we can do that?"

As events continued to unfold, and as the demands of militant and flaunting homosexuals continue to make headlines, Anita and I sat down with our executive director, Ed Rowe, and looked to the future. Anita's question kept ringing in my ears: "What can we do, Bob, to tell the American people how much they mean to us?"

Our office is being flooded with letters from homosexuals who have read *The Anita Bryant Story* and who have seen her on television and followed the events in the media. Stacks of these letters relate how the individuals are turning to Christ and are seeking help. Some of them are struggling and they are pleading for help; others are finding the help they need in caring churches.

We hosted the two-day workshop at our home, and the outcome was a garnering of ideas that include the initial establishment of an office and administrative complex and counseling center at a location to be announced later as plans develop. A toll-free national telephone hotline for purposes of counseling and referral is being put into effect. In time we hope to see a network of counseling centers; mobile counseling units; adoptive-family programs; intensive-treatment facilities; training of pastors and church lay persons for better understanding of homosexuals and their special needs; specialized audio-visual educational programs; farm or ranch complexes for in-depth rehabilitation and whatever other developments God lays upon our hearts to implement. These will be staffed by competent and compassionate Christians trained in counseling and ministering. Help will be offered to those seeking deliverance; we would never force this on anybody.

We envision this as a long-term developing project, but we are wasting no time in setting the wheels in motion to bring all this about.

We have a letter of announcement from "gay" atheists who call themselves a new nonprofit, educational and philanthropic organization established for the purpose of exposing "the monstrosity called 'religion.' " We have information about a "gay" speakers bureau who are organizing to make themselves available to "better inform" the public about homosexuality and Lesbianism as an acceptable alternate life-style. We heard about a session at the American Booksellers Association Convention held in Atlanta where there was a special workshop on how to reach the expanding "gay" market. The San Francisco, California,

Examiner-Chronicle gleefully reports, "Things are happening in the advertising world that would make Anita Bryant squirm. Slowly, sometimes in subtle ways, it is coming out of the closet." It is a known fact that "gay" advertising agencies are springing up, and that "straight" advertisers are beginning to place ads in exclusively "gay" publications, and that "gay" ads are appearing in "straight" magazines. In light of these and other developments, there is no way Anita and I can just sit by idly and do nothing. We believe the American people have spoken and are speaking; we believe God is using others to get the message across to us that there is work to be done, and we are to be in the forefront of doing it.

Legislators, politicians, policemen, teachers, college professors, clergymen, students, mothers and fathers, homosexuals and Lesbians—people from every walk of life—are writing and indicating they share our concern. Los Angeles Police Chief Edward M. Davis declared: "There is no question that homosexuals pose a threat to children. The number of homosexual molestations of young boys has increased just incredibly." San Francisco City Supervisor Dianne Feinstein said, "Gays should not be harassed, but it's reached the point where their life-styles are imposing on others.

"It's a colossal mistake to teach 'gay' sexology in the public schools. You're providing an option for youngsters when they're going through an impressionable period. It could open the door to the worst kind of experimentation. We may live to regret it."

We don't want America's children to have to live to regret it. We receive letters from men in some of this country's prisons. Their anguished cries are not going unnoticed. One such prisoner pleaded with us to continue to get the people of this nation to reexamine their conscience, and for us to "do something."

The editor of the Cleveland, Tennessee, *Daily Banner* commented that this prisoner's letter "may be an expression of one who has tasted the dregs of immorality and lawlessness and knows the consequences of defying laws and standards of righteous conduct.

"He may be one who has witnessed the grim and personally destructive practice of homosexuality where men are thrown together in society's wasteland.

"And he may be a man whose observations and experiences have brought him to the conclusion that immorality and indecency gnaw at a man's spirit and eat away his concept of worth and dignity and consume his hope."

We are grateful to our friends in the Jewish community in many cities who are waging all-out efforts to guard against local laws being changed regarding homosexuals. There are many orthodox rabbis who are fighting the homosexual battle. Rabbi Hecht, spiritual leader in Brooklyn, and president of the Rabbinical Alliance of America, is working to keep New York City from changing its laws. "This would demolish family life . . . ," he declared. "This would destroy communities . . . Leaders of organized religion must come out forcefully with a very strong condemnation of homosexuality so that there is no doubt in the minds of society as to the position of the spiritual and religious clergy leadership of this country.

"What they [the homosexuals] are doing is unnatural and in opposition to biblical precepts which are time-hallowed by Jew and non-Jew alike," he said, quoting many of the Bible passages Anita has used right along.

There is a section of Scripture in the Old Testament which tells of Jehoshaphat, one of the kings of Judah, standing before the people in a time of great national need. After he and his people had prayed to God for deliverance, the king stood and said, ". . . Believe in the Lord your God, so shall ye be established; believe his prophets, so shall ye prosper. And when he had consulted with the people, he appointed singers unto the Lord, and that should praise the beauty of holiness, as they went out before the army, and to say, Praise the Lord; for his mercy endureth for ever" (2 Chronicles 20:20, 21).

As I watch and listen to Anita sing these days, I am reminded of these verses. Anita's faithfulness in "praising the beauty of holiness," is being honored by the Lord. For this we humbly thank God. Anita and I want only to be used of the Lord to accomplish His perfect will. I have to agree with that king of Judah, "His mercy endureth for ever." So be it.

For further information regarding Anita and Bob's continuing efforts to help homosexuals turn from their sin to Christ and to share in Protect America's Children's stand against the militant homosexuals' demand for "gay rights" legislation, please write:

Protect America's Children
P. O. Box 402608
Miami Beach, Florida 33140